Gauri Kund 1.5 KM

A stirring saga of eight who witnessed
Near-death experience in Kedarnath
Natural Disaster

notionpress.com

Gauri Kund 1.5 KM

A stirring saga of eight who witnessed
Near-death experience in Kedarnath
Natural Disaster

EKTAA PATEL

notionpress.com

Notion Press

5 Muthu Kalathy Street, Triplicane,
Chennai - 600 005
First Published by Notion Press 2015

ISBN: 978-93-5206-009-2

I would like to dedicate the book to my Bholenath Shivji, Kaka (my Papa), Mummy, Sister, Bharti, my best friend and to my entire family. They have contributed immensely in shaping the book. Their emotional support and perseverance have been instrumental in completing the book. I also express my heartfelt thanks to my friends and well-wishers who participated in the completion of the book.

Special Thanks to well wishers for their kind support in Rescue Operation

1. My best brothers Bhavesh Patel, Padmanabh Patel, Nimish Patel.
2. My darling sisters Shilpa Patel and Falguni Patel.
3. Nikhil Patel (Jijaji).
4. My bhabhi Purvi Patel, Najuk Patel and Sneha Patel.
5. Dr Kamlesh Patel, Bachubhai Patel and Maniben Patel.
6. Natwarlal Patel Chairman IFFCO (Indian Farmers Fertilizer Cooperative Limited).
7. Tushar Patel, Sandip Patel, Pankaj Patel.
8. Ketan Shah, Dr. Alpesh Shah, Dharmesh Mehta.
9. Chintu Patel & Chirag Patel CEO of Amneal Pharmaceutical, USA.
10. Dr. Rajivkumar Gupta MD Gujarat Narmada Valley Fertilizers Company limited.
11. Officials of Gujarat Narmada Valley Fertilizers Company limited.
12. All officials of Amneal Pharmaceutical.
13. Prabhakarbhai Borole.
14. U S Awasthi MD IFFCO (Indian Farmers Fertilizer Cooperative Limited).
15. All the officials of IFFCO (Indian Farmers Fertilizer Cooperative Limited).
16. Saurabhbhai Patel, Industry Minister Gujarat.
17. Sameer Patel MD of Amos Corporation.
18. Chandubhai Patel and Mahesh Bhai Patel for warm welcome.

19. Rajbir Singh MD of Business Wade.
20. Mehul Chheda.
21. Disaster Managements Team of all States.
22. Medical staff of Jolly Grant Hospital Dehradun.

I would like thanks all friends and relatives who helped us directly or indirectly in our rescue Operation.

Preface

At the outset I would like to confess that this is the first time that I have tried my hand at writing a book. 'Guarikund 1.5 km' is based on a true life story. My family and I were caught in the natural calamity in Kedarnath from which we came out unscathed with more psychological scars than physical ones. The trials and tribulation we underwent, and the hardships and sufferings we overcame inspired me to write the book.

In this book, I have tried to depict the emotional turmoil of the pilgrims in the tussle between life and death during the Kedarnath natural calamity. The firsthand experience of death, destruction and disaster stamped a deep impression on my mind. I saw many deaths and near-death encounters first hand. No one can understand the feelings of those who have lost their near and dear ones. For those who lost their lives in Kedarnath, the only consolation is that they will gain an entry to Heaven.

The traumatic experiences have marked the lives of the survivors. Many have considered it a lesson and many have changed their outlook and attitudes. They have started to treat their lives with more care and cherish their lives better.

Bholenathji has the knack of answering philosophical questions in his own inimitable style. He has given us a new lease of life, which I would like to accept with gratitude and deeper understanding. I feel overwhelmed after surviving the most agonising circumstances.

Today I start my life with a clean slate – one which knows no anger, envy or ego. From now onwards the name of Shivji will be etched in my psyche.

Even after a year, the locals are struggling to make their ends meet. They are still trying to rebuild their houses which were swept away by the uncontrolled fury of nature, for which only we are to be blamed. Homes are still clogged with rubble and refuse. Viewers of media reports would have been sitting secure in their homes while watching the turmoil. But for those caught unawares, they are yet to reconcile with the after-effects of the calamity. People who have suffered such calamities need our generous help. We should come forward and help them in spite of some people discouraging or criticising us.

Acknowledgements

Chintu Patel:

(Amneal Pharmaceuticals USA): Chintu jijaji has traced us at jungle chatti which was most difficult location on the route from kedarnath to gaurikund.he also deputed Prince and Nishant to dehradun to monitor our rescue operation.he also hired a private helicopter which was supposed to rescue us from Fata at Guptakashi.His planning and efforts were priceless. He proved that Family bonding is always first and utmost priority.

P.G Shah:

I really thank PG Uncle for the book. His selfless help and perseverance helped me become competent and qualified to take the big step.

Bharti:

Bharti gave me continuous and unstinted support, constant encouragement and regular nudges to move ahead with the work.

The Angels:

The help and support given by Dayanand, Didi, Taneja Uncle, Richa, Prabhuji and others who were with us through thick and thin. Their help gave us a new lease of life.

Family and relatives:

I thank my entire family and relatives who prayed for our safety and put in unprecedented efforts and time for Operation Rescue. Without their courage and help it would have been impossible to have survived.

Pilots and jawans:

Captains of the choppers, jawans and many others who came from far off places, played their part to take us to safety.

The trekkers:

We thank from our heart, the brave hearts, the trekkers who put their lives on line and rescued us.

I firmly believe that it would have been impossible for me to complete the book without the limitless blessings of Shivji and also grandfather (Dada), Kaka, Mom, and the entire family. Finally, I thank all my friends, well-wishers.

Introduction

Shivji's incomparable and memorable creation which cannot be replicated by anyone, viz, the Himalayas, is considered a heavenly abode. Nature has instilled it with melody, poetry and elegance. The long tracts of green trees, chirping birds and the furiously flowing rivers prove His presence.

The cool breeze, wafting at a leisurely pace, suddenly metamorphosed into gusty winds which heralded torrential rains. The rivers swelled, wiping out all surrounding natural beauty. Meek man with misty eyes can do nothing but be a mute spectator to the wanton destruction wrought by nature's fury. The areas surrounding Shivji's temple at Kedarnath were fully inundated and razed to the ground, except the temple, which remained untouched. What else is it if not the manifestation of truth, making man realise that his life is mortal and momentary? Whenever the cauldron of sin overflows, you experience His divine powers manifested as the witness the fury of nature.

Did you ask how we spent our three days caught amidst
mindless destruction?
Time has never waited for anyone! It only tests us every
moment. No one has ever Tested Time.
The timeless mountains touching the skies bowed in a
second, engulfed by the river as Nature dissolved.
Not easy to appreciate the boundless beauty of nature.
You have to pay the price and risk your life.
Even the Sun lost his saffron hue in the rains.
Or is it due to the fear of destruction that he hid behind
the clouds.

Today is the first day of the journey. I inherited an unshakeable belief in Shankar Bhagwan from my parents. Kaka (Rajnibhai, my Papa) is a devotee of Shankar Bhagwan. He has been offering milk, dahi and water to Shankarji as a ritual every day without fail since he was a child. He is transparent as a person and believes in accruing good karma. He has led a principled life and has brought us up to be so too. One maxim he taught us was: if you are flexible, adjusting and adaptable, you will be liked and accepted by everyone. I have never heard him raise his voice.

The tour was very important for our family. Before the tour we had to cancel the tickets thrice due to unavoidable circumstances. Therefore, this time around, we were determined to undertake the tour come what may. We started preparations in right earnest.

My mother (Hasumatiben) is not as religious as Kaka. She is innocent and has a clear conscience. She was unwilling to take the arduous tour as she was apprehensive. She had heard many stories and experiences of people falling off precipices while riding up on a horse. She felt it was a difficult tour, and she is so soft at heart that she cannot even bear to see the dead body even when there is bereavement in the family. The credit goes to Masi and my sister Jasmina for boosting her morale.

My sister (Jasmina) is like my Mom, performing religious rituals according to her convenience. She has completed 9 out of 12 Jyotirlings; she thought why not complete Kedarnath. She is strong and determined by nature.

PG Uncle and Kaka do business together; they are also best friends. He is quite jovial. He cannot remain hungry even for a minute. He has a penchant for offering three solutions to any problem. He likes to enjoy his life to the fullest. He has a zest for travel and loves the good things of life. He is a self-made person. This time it will be a hat-trick for him to visit Char Dham. It was his idea to do the Char Dham.

Jaate thhe japan pahunch gaye chin (wanted to go to Japan; reached China) - we were originally planning for Nainital but now were heading for Char Dham!

Malti Aunty, Uncle's wife, who is jollier than him, also joined the tour. Though she is diabetic, her will-power is commendable. In spite of an operation on her leg recently, she raised her hand when we took the headcount. Like Kaka she is also an ardent devotee of Mahadevji.

Now we were six of us ready to go. Bini, my friend, is a person of strong will-power. She has no parents; she is like our family member. She is soft at heart but generally holds strong views. She joined us purely as a tourist, for the joy of travelling rather than for any religious reasons. Even her colleagues were surprised.

We booked our tickets. Later Lilaba also joined in. She is very cool and strong-willed but will fall in line if the situation warrants it. She had gone to Kedarnath but had to abort the tour. She wanted to complete the yatra this time. Tickets were booked for her later. Thus, finally, eight of us started preparing for the journey.

Our packing went on till the last minute. Snacks, warm clothes and other essentials. As I am a photography aficionado, I packed photographic paraphernalia. I was excited about capturing the scenic beauty of Uttarakhand.

Our travel agent had prepared a tight itinerary with no leeway as Bini and Jasmina could not get enough leave. He advised us to have a few days extra for any probable exigencies but we could not accommodate it. Our first night stay was at Delhi where we could visit Akshardham. From there on to Haridwar; *aarti* and holy dip at Har Ki Pedi; to Barkot to Yamnotri for *darshan*; Uttarkashi, Gangotri *darshan*; Guptakashi, Kedarnath; overnight stay at Pipalkothi to Badrinath Darshan to Moksha's ladder opening; to taste the Kaliyug era at Shrinagar to Haridwar and back to Mumbai.

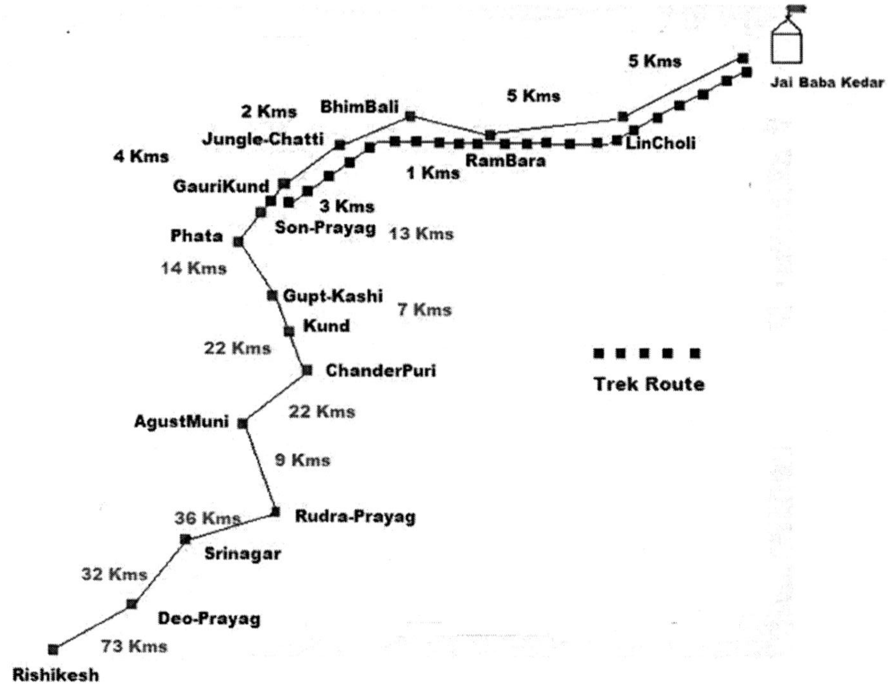
Jai Baba Kedar
5 Kms
5 Kms
BhimBali
2 Kms
Jungle-Chatti
4 Kms
LinCholi
RamBara
1 Kms
GauriKund
3 Kms
Son-Prayag
13 Kms
Phata
14 Kms
Gupt-Kashi
7 Kms
Kund
22 Kms
ChanderPuri
Trek Route
22 Kms
AgustMuni
9 Kms
36 Kms
Rudra-Prayag
Srinagar
32 Kms
Deo-Prayag
73 Kms
Rishikesh

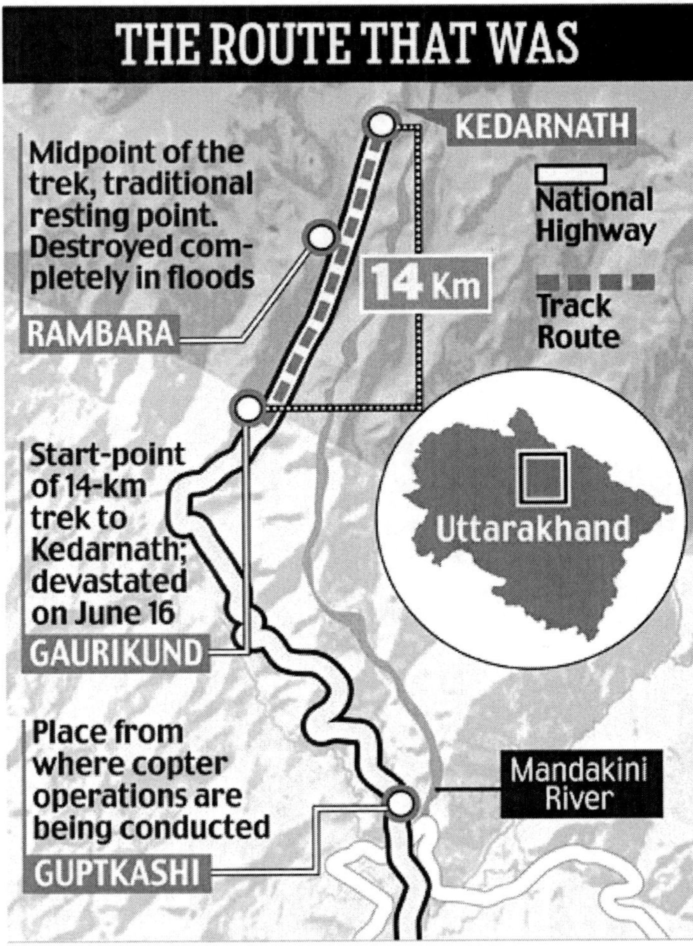
THE ROUTE THAT WAS
KEDARNATH
Midpoint of the trek, traditional resting point. Destroyed completely in floods
RAMBARA
National Highway
Track Route
14 Km
Start-point of 14-km trek to Kedarnath; devastated on June 16
GAURIKUND
Uttarakhand
Place from where copter operations are being conducted
GUPTKASHI
Mandakini River

Contents

Preparation

JUNE 5, 2013 DAY 1

Our tickets for Mumbai-Delhi were for today. Mom, Kaka, Uncle, Aunty, Lilaba and I were to travel by train. Bini and Jasmina would be flying to Delhi later to save time.

We were very excited about the journey, more so me. There was an air of expectancy, anticipation and thrill. I was already capturing in my mind's lens the huge cotton-like snow-covered Himalayan mountain tops and lolling green meadows, eagerly awaiting a '*dekho*' from us. The chants from the excited pilgrims while climbing the mountains were reverberating around the region. Washing the feet of Shankarji, the Alaknanda River gushing forth along the way, creating myriad musical notes, resonated in my mind. The scenes I imagined delighted my very core, and I was thrilled and exhilarated.

However it was tinged with sadness as we could not take Bharti (my childhood friend) along with us. As expected, Bharti came to the station to see me off. She brought 'sohanpapdi' for us. Like some, she did not want us to go as she was apprehensive. We talked shop while she uploaded Ashiqi-2 in my Tablet. Eventually the train got the green signal, and the train whistled and rumbled out the station after the third whistle. The much awaited journey had finally started. Bharti had boarded the local train towards Vile Parle; I was standing at the door. Her train and ours were going parallel. Both the trains were quite apart but I could clearly see the '*I-will-miss-you*' feeling in her eyes!

We made ourselves comfortable in our berths. Moment the train started Uncle took out his new laptop and started playing the songs with enthusiasm. He was very eager to watch video songs of Kareena Kapoor. He is a big fan of hers.

Mom was reluctant about the journey as she was down with the fever, and so was I.

At night we had theplas and pickle for dinner, and then called it a day. I started watching the movie again from where I had paused while everyone else opted to sleep.

Delhi Departure

JUNE 6, 2013 DAY 2

Everybody had a good sleep. It was a lovely morning; all of us got up early. As usual the train was running late. We had home-made theplas for breakfast. I resumed watching the movie. Uncle's enthusiasm about his new laptop had not worn off. I gave him Om Namah Shivay CD to play.

At Kota station, PG Uncle looked out for tea-bhajiawala. The nearest stall was far off. He did not dare get down as he was unsure of the halt time. Ironically the train left after 15 long minutes. Uncle was seen wringing his hands.

We resumed watching Om Namah Shivay CD. Presently the train halted at a signal. I was by the door, feeling the cool air blowing my hair, when suddenly a strong gust of wind swept by, heralding a drizzle. We saw quaint little houses in a village; people were running helter-skelter to keep the flying plastic covers in place on their huts. The kids were returning home from the school frolicking and enjoying their first rains. A whiff of lovely and soothing fragrance wafting from the soil was quite refreshing.

Around 6.30 pm we alighted at New Delhi station. The signs of a gathering storm were very evident. It was very windy. There were all the possibilities of heavy rains. When we came out of the station it was drizzling. Soaking in the first drops of rains, the soil expressed joy by spreading the fragrance of impending rains. It has always been a heavenly experience to witness the first rains of the season. As usual the station was crowded. Finally, we came out of the station, got into our mini bus and headed towards our IFFCO Guest House. After having a hearty dinner and deciding on the next day's programme, we went to bed.

Akshardham Darshan

JUNE 7, 2013 DAY 3

Delhi....da da da da da da dilliii...We were in the capital city. You cannot miss the symbolic India Gate, Parliament Street, Maharashtra Sadan, Metro, white ambassadors with red beacons...the icons which symbolize Delhi. I could see that there was noticeable development in the last 10 years since I had been here.

We visited Lotus Temple, which is a true symbol of unity of different religions. As the name suggests, on each petal is inscribed symbols of all religions expressing unity and harmony, forming a *gulistan*.

After lunch we headed for Akshardham temple. Even as we alighted at the parking lot, we could see the magnificent monument. Its workmanship, its beauty, its grandeur and the cleanliness touched us deeply. As photography is prohibited, we carried the image of its incredible beauty in our minds. It was a sight for the sore eyes.

The temple is so unique and picturesque that one cannot take one's eyes off it. Its hallowed precincts lift you to a higher spiritual level. The architecture and the carvings on the red stone were wonderful and eye-catching. The temple is one of the few well managed temples in India. We did not know about the various shows conducted at the temple. After checking we bought the show tickets accordingly. Many skits in various styles depicting the various important Indian historical milestones and an enlightening short biopic on the Life and Times of Swaminarayan Bhagwan lasting four hours were presented. We also got to see the Indian Heritage cultural shows.

We got engrossed in the Aarti of Ghanshyam Maharaj, which was very uplifting. The colourful musical fountain-show witnessed by thousands was a big hit. It brightened our mood and added to the beauty of the wonderful evening.

The last Darshan - the mosaic and wood-carving of Krishna Leela and Raasleela - were marvellous and out of the world. The momentous memories of Akshardham shall always remain with us.

Thereafter we headed to the house of a family friend, Nandu Uncle. He has been our family friend since Dada's time. He played a perfect host to us. We had a few rounds of mouth-watering gol-gappas. I just could not stop myself and ate much more than my usual. It was *de rigueur* to have it in Delhi. We were waiting for Jasmina and Bini to arrive from the airport. We spent the time together at Nandu Uncle's home gossiping till 2 am. A wonderful day to remember in Dilwalon ki Delhi...

Devbhoomi Haridwar

JUNE 8, 2013 DAY 4

The real journey for Char Dham started today with our entry into Haridwar, the Gateway to Hari's Dham. After having the darshan of and a dip in Ganga Maiya, one automatically becomes eligible for a holy yatra to Char Dham, which includes Yamnotri, Gangotri, Kedarnath and Badrinath.

Delhi to Haridwar is around 208 kms. After the late night discussion at Nandu Uncle's home, it was obvious that we could not wake up early. We managed to start our journey by 10 am.

After a hearty breakfast, we sat in the Tempo Traveller with great enthusiasm, ready for our five hour journey. The excitement though did not last long as we were caught up in a bad traffic towards Haridwar. The tempo snaked through villages' narrow lanes managed to reach the highway. I realised that Mumbai's traffic was much more organised. The traffic was moving at a snail's pace. A little later, we came across two policemen from Uttarakhand Police who were controlling traffic by slowly allowing a few cars to pass through the check post. They flagged our car for a lift. One of them asked our driver, '*Kahan jaa rahe ho?'(Where are you going?)* The driver replied, "Haridwar." The other policeman asked us to make some space for them as they wanted to go to Haridwar too. In return they would give us permission to pass the check post to access the highway. We refused point blank. They were surprised and then furious. Maliciously they diverted our tempo to go by the village roads, denying us the right to take the national highway route. It was very annoying but we were helpless. We had to travel through the narrow lanes which ran parallel to River Gangaji. Sachin, the driver, who knew the area like the back of his palm, proved helpful as he drove us through some breath-taking scenery. The view outside was awesome. The gurgling and bubbling river Gangaji enchanted us. As we were winding through the villages, to keep us occupied, we carried singdana, theplas, khakhra etc. with us. Uncle contemptuously told us that chana is for horses, but later, he had to eat his words, or rather, chana.

We saw every house had a cable connection. Unorganised cluster of wires formed a mess over the narrow lanes of villages, which had low houses. Our car came across one cluster, which was hanging very low. Curiously we peeped out the window to find out a way to pass through. Sachin pulled up the car and coolly asked us to remove a wooden stick with a slit at the top from the back seat. He told us to slip a cluster of wire in the slit and slowly he levered the Tempo forward. We all felt like thanking the policemen for diverting us to canal route. We were feeling blessed to cruise along the canal of river Gangaji. Her slow but steady flow, green meadows and the fresh atmosphere were worth savouring. Coming from the hustle and bustle of the city, the quiet villages and pleasing atmosphere seem quite attractive and enchanting. It was a long but a very delightful journey. Our van crossed mountains after mountains.

We took lunch consisting of simple *daal-bhaat* at a hotel on the way. Finally after a lot of hassle, we reached Haridwar as the clock struck 7 pm. We were eagerly trying to reach Har ki Pedi before the aarti starts at 7. People from all over the world converge on the banks to witness the awe-inspiring aarti. Amongst all the rivers, this is the only one where the aarti is organised on such a large scale. It is worth the effort to attend the aarti. However our hopes were dashed. In spite of our best efforts, we did not reach on time. By the time we reached, the aarti was over and the river was glowing with diyas placed on rose petals scooped in a cup fashioned from leaves. It was lit by the devotees and let to float in the river. It was a divine sight. The music of flowing river, the air resonant with mantras chanted by *Sadhus*, exuberant praising of the holy river by the devotees and ringing of the bells made the environment quite vibrant and spiritual. I was enchanted. The flow was choppy; nobody could stand in its wake. The surging mass of humanity was too large to be accommodated in Har Ki Pedi.

It was 8 pm by the time we completed the darshan. It was once again time to get stuck in the traffic of Haridwar! We left for our hotel but were helplessly caught in a terrible traffic bottleneck. But that was not all. We were told at the hotel that we did not have a booking! They had actually allotted, or rather, auctioned our rooms to other devotees who had converged to attend the Bhagwat week. Nothing can be more annoying than facing so many hardships in a single day. We started our search for a place to spend the night in. We enquired in a number of dharamshalas. Almost all were packed. A few dharamshalas were hot like steam engines. Looking at the condition of the bed sheets and pillows, we thought we would be better off if we spent the night in our car. Eventually we checked in at Hotel Prem Bihari at 12 midnight and dozed off after 1 am. Half of us slept without food.

Barkot Yatra

JUNE 9, 2013 DAY 5

Haridwar, being a pilgrim centre, is abuzz by 4 am, unlike the sleepier big cities, where people tend to wake up later. It was a divine and holy morning in Haridwar. We planned to start at 6 am but could not do so before 7.30 am.

After checking out from the hotel, our tour operator's Haridwar-based manager handed us vouchers and the complete itinerary. Presently Kaka bought my favourite jumbo carton of Amul Kool milk. He also brought Bisleri bottles and Parle-G biscuits to be distributed amongst the poor. Further he bought eight thin sheets of use-and-throw plastic raincoats.Our programme was to visit Barkot. It was the base-point to climb Yamnotri. People arrive at night and start the trek next morning.

Yamnotri is considered an important holy place in Hindu scriptures. The importance lies in the fact that Yamunaji was the better half of Krishnaji. It is mentioned in the scriptures that Yamunaji is the daughter of Lord Sun and sister of Yamdev. According to the Shastras, having bath in the Yamunaji cures one of Thanatophobia - fear of death. The bath also rids the devotees of pain and unhappiness and grants liberation from the cycles of life and death. There are several love stories of Krishnaji and Yamunaji. She is said to have gone around Krishnaji before descending on Earth. Her skin colour was akin to Krishnaji's. Krishnaji had spent his childhood on the banks of Yamunaji. Gangaji and Yamunaji flowed down over the Kalindi Mountains and through the ranges of Himalayas and they flow separately and in parallel. Therefore Yamuna is also known as Kalindi. Gangaji is also known as Himachalendra Tanya as well as Himadri Suta.

The distance being 300 km, we enthusiastically anticipated a picturesque journey. We imagined we would cover the distance in seven hours. We invoked Mataji's name as we headed for Barkot, the base to the holy shrine of Yamnotri. We crossed series of mountain ranges and drank in the surrounding beauty as we crossed the distance we had to pass through Mussorie, the queen of hill stations in Northern India. We were enjoying the wonders of nature and its magic every moment. We thought of enjoying the view of Kempty Falls, its fresh and cool water. Though it was also recommended by our tour operator, the plan had to be abandoned due to a heavy crowd there. It was teeming with children from Delhi who had thronged the hill station enjoying their vacation. It took us nearly three and a half hours just to pass through Mussorie. We saw fresh flowers of myriad hues, which was very pleasing and eye catching, making up for the irritating traffic-jams. We were thrilled by the bounty of nature surrounding us. It seemed that the clouds lowered themselves to greet the flowers on the earth. It was a magnificent sight. Truly it was a sight for the sore eyes. The locals were selling corn (makaai) and boiled spicy chana; eating them enhanced our mood to quite an extent. We were out of Mussorie now. Our guesstimate that we would reach in seven hours went for a toss.

We were passing through many mountain ranges. Suddenly we saw 8-10 kids walking. Kaka beckoned to them and offered biscuits and 1 litre mineral water bottle, which they gulped down in a jiffy. They informed us that they had to trek a few hills to reach their school. We feel exhausted even while travelling in a car; for these boys, trekking was a daily affair. We saw them with moist eyes; we saw happiness in their eyes as they gobbled the biscuits and gulped down water. Those who want to be happy find happiness even in small things in life, while some do not find happiness in spite of lolling in luxury. Less the requirements more are the joys; as it increases, it is an invitation for dissatisfaction.

As we negotiated through the winding roads, dusk descended on us. The natural scenic beauty was so enthralling and invigorating around the curved mountain roads that we felt fresh throughout the journey. We could see the high mountains and pale pink clouds flaking through the night sky. The bulbs seemed like diamonds twinkling and shimmering far away. We were trying to spot the mountain which we will have to climb for Yamnotri. It reminded us of a Hindi film number, '*so gaya, ye jahan, so gaya aasman; so gayi yeh saari manzile, so gaya hai rasta*' (*The nature has slept, the sky has slept; so have the destinations and the roads*). Our car was Queen of the Road as we had the road to ourselves. We felt like kings.

After sometime it was time to refuel the vehicle. The car stopped by at a pump station. Two boys were selling local fruits. Suddenly a boy aged around ten came running towards our car, his hands full of local fruits. We bought some fruits from him. Kaka offered him biscuits. He smiled back and asked timidly, '*kuchh namkeen hai chacha*?'(*Do you have any salty snacks?*) We were all amazed at his gall and could only stare at him. Mom gave him Kachoris. He was delighted and ran towards his elder brother, showing him his 'earnings'. It touched me deeply. Where does the innocence evaporate as we grow up! I realised that happiness lies in all small things; to be happy is our choice. I realised that we should be content with what we have and not worry about what we do not have. The irony is that people do not appreciate what they have. Those who do not have it feel satisfied immensely when they receive it.

We reached Barkot at 10.30 pm. We saw several small hotels. Lots of hotel reps invited us to lodge in their hotels. We reached Nirvana Camp where we had a confirmed reservation. However the driver came back running to say there was no booking in our name! We were shell-shocked. Come on! Not again! The manager came running, informing us that our booking was at 'Camp Nirvana', which was 15 kms further up. That was a huge relief. However the relief was short-lived as our car was about to ram into a bus coming from the opposite direction around a dark and narrow curve. Our hearts stopped. Luckily, with the blessings of Goddess Yamunaji, we escaped. We breathed easy and felt relieved. That was a close shave! We advised the driver to drive slowly. We were eagerly waiting to reach our Camp.Camp Nirvana is not a hotel but a group of tents with all the usual facilities. After the hectic travel and simple dinner, we slept. We decided to start by 5 am the next day for Yamnotri Darshan.

Yamnotri Darshan

JUNE 10, 2013 DAY 6

It was the day to visit the Yamnotri shrine. As we wanted to leave at 5 am, we were served hot water for bathing from 4 am – this also served as a wake-up call. We were ready by 5.30 as we had to drive for 2 hours and trek 7 km trail thereafter.

The setting of the Camp was beautiful; the gurgling water of Yamnotri, nearby mountain ranges, sun rising with a halo of rays, coyly trying to come out of the clouds beyond the mountains, chirping birds and flower beds along the river with dew-drops on the petals, twinkling like diamonds had created an ethereal ambience. As the sunrays grew stronger, sunflowers open up their petals lazily to soak in the divine atmosphere. The birds shook themselves languorously as they came out of the warm and cosy nest. Add to it the music emanating from the river, and I was delighted! The sprinkling spray from the river on the flowers made them dance to the tune of the wind. The climate was very chilling and the morning was as fresh as a bud.

We had a nap in the car. We reached the base point Janki Chatti, where our car was mobbed by a number of doliwalas and horsewalas. They were very aggressive, shoving each other as they tried to thrust their ID cards into our hands. We were surprised. The system was: once you accept an ID card, you have to finalise the horsewala it belonged to. Our driver advised us not to accept any cards till we finalised the deal.

Uncle was the first to hire a horse and ride off. Kaka, Jasmina, Bini and I decided to walk it up. However the driver vetoed the idea as it would take longer and the path was very difficult. Further, other horsewalas would make it difficult to walk. Kaka agreed and hired the horses. Bini was thrilled at the prospect of riding a horse. Mom was too scared to walk the full stretch. She along with Lilaba and Aunty opted for the doli. It took Kaka nearly an hour to finalise one. Finally we were ready to go.

Presently we heard the shrieks of Jasmina for help. We looked back to see her petrified face. Due to fear her face had turned red, and she started sweating. We could not stop laughing as she was walking with a leg entangled in the stirrup of the pony. She outright rejected the horse. The horsewala said the pony is of racing breed. Every one tried to convince her that the pony was just being mischievous as he was young and so naughty too; she reluctantly acquiesced.

The entire stretch was fenced by iron railings for the safety of the pilgrims. There were some alternatives to walking; one can hire the horses, or a doli, or there were even pittuwalas, who lugged the pilgrims sitting on a bamboo basket on their backs with a cloth running through the basket and over the forehead. Pittu is a basket fashioned from bamboo sticks. It is very strenuous for the person carrying. However, it is their bread and butter. The scenario was very lamentable and unfortunate. The work is limited to four months a year. All the young and able from the nearby villages take up the profession to earn extra money. The profession is short-lived as the knees stop functioning after 30 years of age due constant pressure and wear and tear.

As we started moving ahead, my horse constantly turned back. The handler explained that his brother was left behind; he wanted to remain with him. It made me appreciate that animals too have feelings. I realised that man has become more practical whereas the animals still let feelings govern them.The natural setting was marvellous. Nearby the river was charting its own path making soothing gurgling sound, which was music to my ears.

And guess what? Traffic was just as heavy here. The only difference was the component of the traffic; it was a medley of humans (pilgrims) and horses. The horse owners and doliwalas would not allow the people to walk freely. They would barge into them from either side of the road. It was a two-way traffic, so people had to walk in a single file. The driver's stand was vindicated. We were moving from one mountain to another. The clouds, as if exhausted from roaming, decided to be comfortable and settled over the mountains.

Looking back I could see as if a fair of horses was under progress. The importance of Char Dham involves human beings converging there. The faith is very strong; be it a child or a wizened old man, they would rustle up the required strength to reach all the Dhams.We have seen police controlling the vehicles. The police here helped streamline and control the traffic of horses. Police managed the man-horses show well - thanks to liberal usage of the 'danda'.

At last, we reached Yamnotri after wading through the mass of human beings. as pilgrims were taking bath in the hot water springs. It is a miracle how hot water springs flowed adjacent to chilling water. Even the hard-core atheist would be forced to ponder on the phenomenon and reading the scriptures to find the truth. Faith is very personal as Hindus deify the God carved out of stone, which others may scoff at. It was a huge congregation of people with immense faith. Invoking the name of Yamunaji, pilgrims were having frequent dips in the hot springs. Everywhere there was hectic activity of bathing, people changing clothes, others manning their luggage and some managing their wayward kids. The noise disturbed the serenity of the atmosphere. Perhaps after six months (of being closed to pilgrims), the noise alerted Yamunaji of her oncoming devotees. As it was peak season, the temple premises were teeming with people. People of all ages had thronged the entrance. We had a satisfying darshan of Yamnotri. The whole atmosphere was very spiritual. The water in the springs was so hot that even the rice would get cooked in just two minutes - people were taking it home as Prasad. Several pundits were performing puja, chanting Mantras and Shlokas. The feeling was very overwhelming and blissful.

We just sprinkled hot water on ourselves chanting Mataji's name. However, Kaka and Uncle had a dip on behalf of all of us. We were tired after travelling 14 km. Whereas after the bath, Kaka and Uncle were feeling fresh.

Women had lowered their colourful bandhani saris studded with small mirrors in Yamunaji River, creating an illusion of floating diamonds twinkling on the river. I personally feel that it is better that the saris are given to some needy women who could wear it, thus accruing triple benefit: expressing our devotion to Mataji, earning good karma and serving the needy. People who are searching for value for money will be triply benefitted. Also nature gets disturbed when the fish get caught in the saris unwittingly and die, thus polluting the river, which should not be allowed. Pilgrims should ensure that the river water remains clean and potable.

We reassembled at 5 pm; when we reached the parking lot, the driver was not traceable. Another driver informed us that the brake oil had leaked, and it was in no condition to go to the Camp. "Your driver is not taking due care," they pointed out and we were dismayed.Later our driver came and assured us that we shall somehow reach the Camp safely. The days here are fresh and stimulating, which cannot be said of the nights as they are not safe. When we returned, we did not find anyone on the way, which made the atmosphere eerie and bizarre. Nobody uttered a word till we reached the Camp at 10 pm. Though we enjoyed the ride, we were tired; we ordered dinner in the room as we could not make ourselves get up. Nearby, Yamunaji was running to the tune of her own perennial soft music. The music induced us to sleep in no time.

Uttarkashi Yatra

JUNE 11, 2013 DAY 7

We slept well with Yamunaji's music in the background. We got up to the same musical score. In Mumbai we would not have woken up before 10 am; however here we were up at about by 7 am. thanks to the surfeit of pure oxygen available all around us. The music was very soothing as it made us fresh and energetic. As the birds chirped around, we saw the woolly clouds had covered the mountains. We enjoyed watching the mountain playing hide and seek. The sun also joined in the fun.

The music was beckoning us. The beauty presented to us by the Great Naturalist on a golden platter has to be seen to be believed, and was sight for the Gods. It was so alluring that Jasmina, Bini and I thought of going closer to river.

We had to leave for Uttarkashi. However Jasmina, Bini and I went for a photography session. And as we approached the river, the rain also joined the game. The yellow, pink and reddish flower beds showed us the way. My eyes were getting overwhelmed with the scenic beauty of Yamnotri; I ran out to shoot every scene in all possible angles I managed to capture some of the best photographs in my life. I was happy and fortunate. It is god's creation, humans cannot even imagine it.

We started off on our journey to Uttarkashi, fondly called as UK in Uttarakhand, through the narrow roads carved out from the mountains, singing and making merriment. On the way we kept ourselves busy by offering biscuits to children and sadhus. Kaka has always taught us to do good karmas.

Work done with faith and perseverance brings sure success. The sadhus to whom we were offering biscuits were determined to complete the Char Dham on foot. Uncle, his journalistic instincts coming to the fore, started interviewing them: Wherefrom have you come? Where are you going? Which Dham have you covered? Do you prefer anything else to biscuits? Hearing the answers, Uncle's train of thoughts got triggered. Extending the logic of the proverb 'as you sow so shall you reap' Uncle said to Kaka: "As you are offering biscuits, they shall repay in the same coin when you are hungry in Heaven. However, I like gulab jamun as I have a sweet tooth. Therefore, henceforth we shall offer gulab-jamuns to all the sadhus so I will be served the same delicacy in Heaven."

Everybody had a hearty laugh. Aunty, annoyed, ordered Uncle to look for a cook who can make the delicacy while we go for the Darshan. Kaka continued with the gulab-jamun rhetoric. Aunty cautioned Kaka not get carried away. She remarked that she knew Uncle very well, If Uncle does not see any sadhu, he would gulp it off one by one on the pretext that it would get spoilt otherwise. Everybody laughed again, making the journey enjoyable.

The car was cruising its way through great distances. The peals of laughter resounding in the valley were abruptly shattered by a loud blast emanating from behind, indicating a tire burst. The driver applied the brake with full force, and the car bumbled its way erratically, thudding to a stop, fortunately toward the mountain side. There was pandemonium in the car. We were frightened to the core. Everybody was stunned, our pulses raced; some missed heart beats. We involuntarily clutched the seats in front of us for support. Small stones had strewn all around. We again had a close shave. While the driver got down, we were all abuzz and agog with numerous queries. The driver advised us to get down and remain near the valley side to avoid falling stones. Fortunately, the drivers of the two cars coming from behind turned out to be our driver's friend. They helped him replace the old tyre with a new tyre along with a new ring. We needed to be cautious as they were the smallest and porous mountains in the world and had the propensity to crumble down even at the slightest sound. Uncle confirmed that these were the 'youngest' mountains, making it difficult to travel through.

From here on the limits of Gangaji had started. Gangaji was twice as aggressive and choppy compared to Yamunaji, roaring like a lion. Gangaji was spraying the water on us as we raced alongside. The flow was bounded and limited by the mountains, but still she managed to slosh, swash and splurge, trying to overcome the banks. Like a precocious child, she was full of energy, singing and dancing along the way, fearlessly overcoming any and everything in its wake.

We reached Uttarkashi before dusk, breaking our jinx of always reaching late. Even before checking-in at the hotel, everyone except Jasmina and I opted to roam around the local market to shop. I was feeling a bit feverish. Jasmina stayed back to take care of me. Gradually my fever increased as Gangaji increased her pace. The temperature shot from 101 deg F to 102 reaching 103. I was as hot as hell. As it reached 103, Kaka and others returned. We consulted the doctor on phone who advised medicines and cold press on the forehead continuously till the fever subsided. Everybody was worried and was enquiring about my wellbeing. They assured me that if by tomorrow the fever did not subside, we all shall rest. The staff of Shiv Parivar took good care of me. They brought hot potion given in fever. They were on their toes till midnight. Uncle brought The Shrimad Bhagwat Gita and recited a chapter.

The location of the hotel was exotic. I could easily access Gangaji and dip my feet. There was a garden overlooking Gangaji. I had planned to do meditation on the adjacent bank like rishi munis would do in the vicinity of a river. The plan obviously fizzled out due to the fever.

Gangotri Yatra

JUNE 12, 2013 DAY 8

It was a day to pay homage at the Gangotri shrine. Sachin, our driver, advised us to be ready by 6 am. Everybody enquired about my health but I was quite determined to continue with the tour. We left as planned.

Last night the driver had taken others to Shankarji's Mandir. The folklore goes thus: Parshuram did severe penance, which gladdened the heart of Shankarji who descended to the Earth to shower blessings on him personally. Some folks believe it to be one of the 12 Jyotirlings. There was a totem pole purported to be Parshuramji's. As Jasmina and I wanted to have a darshan, Kaka advised the driver to halt for 10 minutes. Before we reached the temple, the driver had lined up the car in a kilometre queue at the only petrol pump there, costing us an hour. The road leading to Kedarnath was blocked due to a landslide. However, when we assured the police that we were heading for Gangotri, they allowed us to go. It seemed traffic was not going to leave us even for a moment anytime. The roads were narrow with lots of hair-pin bends thrown in. However the scenic beauty left us breathless. Though the road was narrow, all the drivers were driving their car fast, including our driver. The serpentine roads and crossing of the mountains one after another was breath-taking.

Gangotri means the source of Gangaji, whose other name was Bhagirathi, which was prevalent for a long time. It is an important river in the Hindu Scriptures. There was one king, Bhagirath whose forefathers were living under a 'curse', that they would not achieve liberation even after their deaths. As a result, their spirits were roaming aimlessly. Only Gangaji was capable of liberating Bhagirath's forefathers. Gangaji's flow was so furious that it would wipe out the entire earth. Only Mahadev could control the velocity of Gangaji through his jata. King Bhagirath knew about it and that is why he did severe penance and requested Shankarji to liberate his forefathers and also for the good-will of Kaliyug people, by bringing Gangaji to Earth. Gangaji was reluctant to appear on earth, worried about her purity being compromised, when Shivji assured Gangaji that the wise sages, saints and devotees will bath in her holy waters resulting in her purification. Against her wish Gangaji bowed to the request of Shankarji to appear on Earth. Gangaji agreed to wash off the sins of the people with a clause that her purity would remain untouched. Shankarji entwined his huge jata and reigned in Gangaji so that it flowed serenely. Hence Shivji is also known as Gangadhar. The forefathers of Bhagirath, wherever they were present, thus were released from the curse and were able to merge into the sea. Hence one dip in Gangaji is said to open up the doors of heaven. Despite the fever, my avidity for going to heaven enticed me to go to Gangotri.

Suddenly we had a head-on collision with a Zen car coming in the opposite side, navigating a blind curve at break-neck speed. Our car was towards the valley side and veered off dangerously close to the precipice as the driver stepped on the brake with full force, showing great skill. The car thudded to a stop just at the edge. The incident was over in the blink of an eye. There was hardly any time to react. There was no time for thinking or understanding. What's happening? We were on tenterhooks. We wondered why we were being subjected to near-calamities all the time. It could have snuffed out our lives in a second. For all we knew, by now we would have been in the lap of Gangaji. The accident was terrifying as our car's six out of eight axles had broken. We wondered what will happen and how we were going to reach our hotel. The driver saved the day and our lives. But though we were safe and secure, we were stranded.

Man's life is always on an edge. He loves his life and shall go to any lengths to save it. To attain emancipation we take a dip in the Gangaji, but nobody wishes to land in the lap of Gangaji soon. Strange are the ways of man!

After sometime, with some improvisation, we started again and reached Gangotri safely with no further hiccups. Unlike Yamunaji, here we can take the car right up to the temple. While walking towards the temple, we saw a foreign group including girls carrying back packs looking to hire a guide for Gaumukh, which, being still higher up, is out of bounds for the usual pilgrims. I was surprised that they study the Hindu Scriptures and travel thousands of miles from their country to experience it first-hand. They accept the new religion whole-heartedly and sincerely. They easily took the decision to trek to the upper reaches, which we find difficult to take. Voluntary acceptance of a religion is more sustainable than the forced one, which tends to make one resistant.

After walking a few steps, we reached the Gangotri Temple. We had a wonderful darshan.

The crowd was less here than in Yamnotri. It is a common ritual among the pilgrims to collect the holy water from the flowing Ganga in a bottle or a plastic container. We too collected some. It is used for performing puja. It is holy. Gangajal has a peculiar property - water does not get contaminated in the bottle for years. There are no bacteria nor does it smell for years on end. The fact would make even the atheist believe in god and the scriptures. No other river in the world possesses such properties as Gangajal. It is a subject ripe for research. Can anyone explain why mosquitoes and insects do not survive in Gangajal?

Bhagirath Maharaj had done penance at the point where the road leading to Gaumukh begins. There is an ancient image of him. The road to Gaumukh is very difficult for the pilgrims. Regular pilgrims return from here.

We had taken a pair of clothes with the intention of taking a dip in Gangaji. It seemed we would have to take it back unused. The river water was raging and so chilling that you cannot dip your foot for more than 10 seconds; you may start freezing. If you dip your hand, you feel as if it is in the freezer. We could see the snow melting from the distant mountains and turning into a river.

As I was feverish I was warned against going anywhere near the bank, which seemed counter-productive. My tour would not be complete till I dipped my feet. Mustering courage, I let Gangaji wash my feet, cupped some Gangajal in my hands and sprinkled over my head. Others followed suit. Now it was Uncle's turn. Before he could dip his feet, Kaka challenged him. "If you can manage to stand for a minute, I shall offer you Rs 100,000." Uncle excitedly said with false bravado, "Rajnibhai, do not back out!" Kaka said, "Hundred per cent! I give you my word."

Uncle withdrew his feet the moment he placed it in the water, developing cold feet, remarking, "I love life more than money!"

He was not exaggerating. Gangaji's water was freezing cold. However, a few pilgrims had gathered courage to pour a glass of water on their heads, as well as on their children's. Hats off to their faith and courage. Although they were shivering and their teeth were chattering, it is a matter of overcoming the inertia! My fever remained steady. After Shankarji, Gangaji's water is the purest; no wonder Gangajal is used for Abhishek in Kedarnath. The devotees fill Gangaji's water from here as it is the cleanest and purest. No, people have not been able to contaminate the water here as yet.

We performed puja with the help of a punditji. He twined the sacred thread around the Gangajal bottle, sought liberation for our seven generations like Bhagirath. Anybody would get drawn in the flow as it was steadily increasing. The water was muddy because of heavy rains in upper reaches of Gaumukh areas. After some time we saw the flow becoming ferocious.

While returning we had a plate of tasty chhole bhature. The chilled climate added zing to its flavour. It was simply fascinating. We started our return journey after the wonderful meal. As usual roads were jammed due to the traffic. The brook etched its way through the hills. Men made use of the stones to fashion a narrow bridge. The buses from both sides jammed the road. How much time it would take to clear off was anybody's guess. Luckily we were first in the line. People advised our driver to drive the car slowly. It was very risky. Our heart beat faster. But the driver was very confident. He just raced away and crossed the stone bridge. As soon as our car crossed, the edge of the bridge broke, disturbing the stones which flew in all directions! Hats off to him that he showed enough presence of mind and got us out safely, else it would have been catastrophic. Pilgrims behind us must have got stranded for hours on end. The traffic line lengthened. After sunset, it was pitch dark. The car raced down the deserted road with the broken axles.

We proceeded further taking God's name. When we were 4 kms shy of our hotel, the sky opened up with unabated fury, taking us unawares, plunging us in complete darkness and raising the river levels, making us feel uneasy.

There was no network for the whole day. As I was down with high fever, Bharti was eagerly waiting to talk out of concern for me. When we spoke, she informed me that there was landslide in Gangotri, thankfully after we left. As our schedule was tight, we could not have afforded a single day's delay entailing missing darshans, leading to an incomplete tour. We somehow managed to complete Gangotri yatra.

Finally, it was another night's halt at Hotel Shiv Parivar. We were exhausted and went off to bed early.

Guptakashi Yatra

JUNE 13, 2013 DAY 9

From Uttarkashi our base camp was Guptakashi, en route to Kedarnath. We were ready by 6 am. The driver went to collect the repaired axles and tyre from the mechanic. Without our knowledge Kaka had made lunch arrangements for 25 needy people. We could only leave by 9 am.

We wove our way through many mountain ranges. The scenic beauty was unique. We could see the mountains through a thin sheet of ice melting continuously. After being hidden for six months, the mountains were eagerly looking out for sun rays. We breathed deep to inhale the fresh fragrance emanating from the soil after the first rains. The green grass was gasping with joy. The melting snow was sparkling like diamond, nourishing the grass and the budding flowers. Small leaves were germinating from the dry bed of trees. Adding to it were the whistling winds creating a bracing and stimulating atmosphere. Here time works more leisurely and everybody awaits their turn. We need to apply it in our life. One should not be impatient, nor gloat at others' bad times.

I don't have enough words to describe the unique beauty of the place. As we were in Devbhumi, we were surrounded by truth and purity. To appreciate it, one should have a pure heart.

From here on it was a single lane all along. Our car was racing past, replying to the whistling winds. The contrast between the rust-coloured tall and wide trunked trees and the soil with lighter shade was picturesque. The low clouds hovering at a leisurely pace over the tiny villages added to the overall charm. It was pleasing to watch farmers ploughing the paddy fields in their demarcated areas. The flowers were looking fresh after a long period of snowing. The pure and excellent quality of air added zest and spring to our mood.

The beauty around us was so enticing that we did not feel the drudgery of travelling long distances even rapidly. I could even meditate. Along the way we continued our daily routine of distributing biscuits whenever we saw sadhus or needy people. While giving the biscuit, Bini called out to the sadhus lyrically, as if disturbing their meditation like Menka would do. We had a good laugh; even the driver could not help himself.

The darkness enveloped us. Many villagers come for the Char Dham Yatra. They make themselves comfortable in some cosy nook. Along the way, mess operators were trying to flag us down to have dinner. Opposite the mountain ranges were single floor tenements. Here they have only four months available to earn as the rest of the year it is inhabitable and inhospitable terrain. They convert their houses into dhabas. Children also chip in. Man has to earn his bread any which way. There was a lot of din and noise with the loud blaring of CDs playing Shankarji's bhajans along the way.

Our car passed the village, in the middle of which was located Table Land where our camp was situated. It was pitch dark. The road leading to the camp was pothole-ridden, on a precipice and steep. The car made slow progress; two steps forward and one step backward. It seemed as if the car was fearful and hesitant of the dark. Uncle has Nyctophobia - fear of darkness. He frantically searched for a torch in the bags. The ladies thought we got misled; for a moment even the driver got confused. On calling the hotel, we got the confirmation and were told to drive further and look out for a lit bulb as we climb up. Now all eyes were looking for the bulb, which will light up and defuse the darkness and our fear. Again we called as we could not locate the bulb. He advised us to drive further up and not to worry. We braved the potholes, and presently the bulb lightened our anxiety by dispelling the darkness.

Everybody was relieved to see the bulb. It lit up a ray of hope, giving peace of mind. One should not back-track in fear of darkness; two steps forward will surely lead to enlightenment.

Everyone complained about the location. It was freezing cold. We reached the dining hall, where many insects of various hues had gathered attracted by the light. We saw others preparing for the Kedarnath journey the next morning. There was tension in the air. We were sipping piping hot soup and listening to them, "Must be very cold. We must carry clothes." We thought we would get up at our leisure, but we were told to be ready by 5 am.

Everyone went to sleep, anxious about having to wake up early the next day.

Kedarnath Yatra

JUNE 14, 2013 DAY 10

As per the itinerary, we were to climb the Kedarnath shrine today, stay on the hill overnight and come down the next morning. Accordingly we had to leave the tent by 5 am.

Everybody got up by 4 am. Peeping through the tent I could see lot of hectic activity all round the place. Some group had already left. When I came out shortly after, the beautiful scene made me gasp for breath! It was beyond anybody's imagination. I could see that our tent was surrounded by mountains in three concentric curves, with the river flowing in between. As I came out from the tent the sun was rising between the mountains. The river was coursing in a zigzag path through the mountains, which contained the flow. The mountain had created a boundary like a loving brother and led the river like a doting father from one range to another in a circular motion. Sun was peeping through the clouds periodically. The snow clad mountains and the chirping birds! Aha Aha Aha...Wow! It was the most beautiful sight in my life and shall remain etched in my heart forever. Nobody felt like leaving the place as it was charming, bewitching and appealing. The morning was in its full bloom and glory. Previous night all of us were thinking whether we should ask our tour operator to change the venue. However, we appreciated his choice after witnessing the beauty of the place.

The location of the hotel where we stayed was beautiful but was situated on the difficult higher reaches. It is said that to achieve good things in life, we need to tread the difficult path. Then beauty is experienced and appreciated even more. It loses its charm if it is easily obtained.

Everyone was overjoyed by the beauty. Bini, Jasmina and I already decided to stay for two days next time around. We noted that the weather was very ephemeral around here. A while ago you were enjoying the rains and now you are basking in the sun, manifesting its power in all its glory.

Before leaving we got into a discussion as to whether we should carry our luggage along or not. The local tent people were of the opinion that we must carry the luggage along with us. But our driver advised us to take only the essential things in a small handbag and leave the rest behind as we were suppose to come back next night anyway. Eventually, after much discussion, we took the decision of leaving the luggage behind. We left for our next stop - Gaurikund.

We left from Guptakashi at 5 in the morning. Mom, Lilaba and Aunty were to be lifted in a helicopter while the rest of were to go on horses.

Plan A: We reached the helipad. Service had been halted. We got to know from the management of the airlines that they were not sure whether services will be resumed any time because of inclement weather conditions. Obviously the plan did not work, as we just could not go on the assumption that helicopter service would resume soon. If the flight did not take off at all, then how would Lilaba, Mom and Aunty reach Kedarnath?

Plan B: We all headed to Gaurikund and decided to hire doliwalas and horses. Again the plan failed; Mom had an altercation with Kaka. She felt that she was purposely not being sent by helicopter as Kaka wanted to save money. She was scared to go by doli or horse. As we were proceeding further, we saw another helipad; we went to check the availability.

Aunty had a leg operation recently. Due to Lilaba's age and Mom's anger, we went to enquire about the service. The management agreed to accommodate all three ladies immediately when they heard about their problems and rest of us by 2 pm. We were happy. The copter had gone on a sortie and would be back shortly. We paid the money and got the boarding passes as well. Mom was delighted; so were we to see her happy.

They started discussing where they would land and whether they would remember the name of the hotel. We advised them not to wait for us; just go to the hotel. Mom and Lilaba were a certainty for air travel. As they were moving we were informed that the copter service has been suspended for some time. Oh God; your plans are inscrutable! We were disheartened. Bini, Jasmina and I were looking forward to go by the copter. Even after half an hour turned to two hours, there was no progress as they had suspended the services indefinitely. We bombarded the management with pointed questions but they had no answers. We were worried whether the delay would send our itinerary for a toss.

Presently we were informed that doliwalas and horsewalas had gone on sudden strike as they felt their business was getting affected due to the deployment of helicopter services. It was afternoon. We got anxious; what would happen next? We were waiting for the next call. In answer to our pointed question, we were told by the management that hopefully the strike would get over shortly. We kept our fingers crossed. God was testing us. We were worried whether we shall have Darshan! As the schedule was tight we wondered how we shall manage the future programmes. It was 2 pm now.

The sun was shining brightly, which was conducive to flying, but we cannot go against Bholenath's wishes. Presently we were hungry, and Uncle more so. This led the chef in Uncle to come to the fore. He got the bright idea of cooking for us. We bought some onions, capsicum and tomatoes from the nearby local vendor. He requested a restaurant owner to lend some utensils and basic spices and condiments for cooking. The dhabawala was kind enough to provide the rotis. We loved the preparation as it was good.

It is said that patience always bears fruits. However, our patience for services to resume was wearing thin. We lost hope and decided to turn back when we heard nothing till 4 in the evening. People had been waiting for the copter services for three days to no avail. In spite of firm bookings, the ephemeral weather condition forced the service providers to err on the side of caution. People were fed up with the uncertainties and decided to go on the horse. In fact, we had our booking at Kedarnath for today. Finally we realised that all our plans had failed and we had to go back to square one again.

We decided to spend the night in Sitapur, which was on the way to Kedarnath. It was like falling from the fire into the frying pan. We were again harassed by the ubiquitous traffic. The buses were standing face to face, waiting to see who would blink first. From past experience, we knew we would lose at least 2 hours here. It was a total waste of a day. We were clueless about what was happening around.

The driver said, "As we have lost the day, to make up, we shall leave tomorrow early by 4 am so we can return early in the evening, and day after tomorrow continue as per itinerary. We shall go for the darshan of Dhari Devi en route to Badrinath." We enquired, "Dhari Devi?" The driver was surprised that we were not aware of the importance of Dhari Devi. He continued, "It is mandatory to have the Darshan of Dhari Devi after Kedarnath. Her shrine is one of the 108 Shaktipeeths and she is the better half of Shankarji, because of which he is also known as Ardhanareshwar. Like Shankarji, her temple is also located on the banks of Alaknanda. The folklore suggests that many years ago during the floods, her idol was swept away and got stuck amongst the stones near the banks. Villagers heard someone crying and ran toward the source – divine voice was coming from the idol.

From Dharimataji's idol a voice came expressing her desire to be installed at the same place where it was found. The villager's did as advised. As the incident happened in Dharigaon, it was decided to name her Dhari Devi. She is the incarnation of Kali Mata. As per instructions, the temple was built open on all sides. This shrine does not have a dome. The locals have built a bridge across Alaknanda River to facilitate easy access to the temple. Photography is strictly prohibited. Kalimata is in sleeping pose; her upper half is in Dhari while the lower part is in Kalimadh in Rudraprayag. In Rudraprayag they perform puja of the Shri Yantra. Dhari mataji's idol is installed on a 20 ft stone. In the morning she is worshipped in the form of a child (Bal Swaroop), in the afternoon as a young woman, and in the evening as an old woman. You need to see the Devi to believe it.

In 1882 it was decided to shift the idol to accommodate the construction of a dam, which was severely opposed by the locals. All the same the administration decided to shift the idol. As they started shifting the temple, a sudden flood resulted in loss of life and property. Hell hath no fury like a woman scorned. Once she is disturbed, her rage has no limits, and hence Shankarji is close by to reign her anger. Their togetherness helps in avoiding any untoward incidents. We do not want to witness Rudra Swarupa nor Rudra Tandav, do we?

Everybody was lapping the folklore with wide-eyed interest and pin-drop silence. It seemed they were watching a bioscope of Dhari Devi's life and times. As we were religious minded we believed the folklore as the driver was religious too. It is up to you to believe the God carved out from the stone is God or just a stone. Those who have experienced God swear by Him.

Presently we reached Sitapur. Kaka and Uncle made arrangements for boarding and lodging, which they could manage to find in the first attempt. We had a simple dinner and tried to sleep early as we had set an alarm for 3 am. I had no appetite and so I slept early.

Kedarnath Darshan

JUNE 15, 2013 DAY 11

From 2 am itself, there was hectic activity as pilgrims knocked on each other's doors, calling the names of their group members to get ready. Some groups were already off to Gaurikund, en route to Kedarnath. We got up at 4 am.

We left at 5.30 am. Before we could settle in our tempo, we were greeted by strong gale and rains accompanied by lightning. It was like a 100-member musical orchestra. We invoked the name of Bholenathji. We thought as we were early we would not face much traffic. But that was not to be. There was no respite from traffic right from the word go. On the one side was the narrow road carved out from the mountains and on the other side was Alaknanda flowing in all its glory and fury. They were allowing 100 cars to Gaurikund at a time. We had to wait till they returned, thereby avoiding congestion at Gaurikund. It would set us back by two hours. Some tried to snatch forty winks. Every minute was like an hour. I was getting impatient to have darshan of Kedarnath.

Bini and I were gossiping when suddenly Bini asked Kaka, "Yesterday we heard about Dhari Devi. Please tell me the importance of Kedarnath." We chided her, reminding her that she was an atheist and just a tourist. Kaka said, "Keep quiet; do not harass her." He asked, "Do you know of the Pandavas who fought the battle?" Bini replied, "Yes."

When Pandavas fought the battle, they inadvertently killed many innocent people, which unwittingly made them big sinners. For repentance they sought liberation from their sins by seeking the darshan of Shankarji, which will wash away all their sins, making them eligible for entry into the Heaven. The abode of world's greatest sympathiser Shankarji is in the Himalayas. Pandavas left Kashi for the Himalayas via Haridwar. When they neared the ranges, Shankarji played hide and seek with them. Saddened Dharmaraja beseeched Shankarji for the darshan as they had committed the sin of killing innocent lives. Is it the reason for your hiding? However we shall find you as we would not be liberated from the sins till we have your darshan. As you are hidden here, the place shall be known as Guptakashi.

The search led them to Gaurikund without any result; undeterred they walked to Kedarnath. Suddenly Sahdev and Nakul saw a herd of buffaloes. Shankarji was not willing to give darshan so easily. Shankarji was one of them. Bhim ran forward and stood akimbo, enabling passage of all animals easily but the buffalo! The trick worked to a nicety. Shankarji was sort of 'filtered out'. However, Shankarji gave him the slip; Bhim was on hot pursuit. He somehow got hold of the tail, which he pulled up hard with great force. To escape from the grip, Shankarji rammed into the soil, and his head came out in Rudranath! The upper portion is installed in Pashupatinath, Nepal, the legs in Tungarnath and abdomen in Mahamaheshswar.

Shankarji presented himself in his full regalia. Shivji informed the Pandavas that henceforth he will be residing here in the form of a triangular Shivling. As they received liberation from all sins, He offered to emancipate the common man also. Bhim realised that Shankarji must be hurt, so he applied ghee to his sore tail. Hence pilgrims offer ghee to Shankarji. Till today pilgrims believe that Shankarji and Mataji reside here. Mataji takes a daily dip above Kedarnath temple in Chorabari Talav. Talav is guarded by snakes, traces of which are found even today. The road to Heaven used by the Pandavas is called Swarga

Rohini. Vishnuji advised Shivji to remain here in his original form for the welfare of the people.

Listening to our story, the driver added that he had heard that earlier all the Char Dhams were connected by the shortest route, which enabled the Punditji to perform puja at all the Char Dhams in a day. The route has been obliterated due to erosion. Nobody knows about it since his death.

We were all engrossed in the story. We came across a blanket seller. Kaka beckoned him and negotiated for a dozen blankets. The vendor was happy to get the first deal of the morning. We wondered why Kaka was buying blankets, but he did not respond to our queries.

It was time to cross the second and maybe the last stop before reaching Gaurikund. On the way Kaka offered two blankets to two sadhus. They were overjoyed and showered blessing on him. We got our answer.

My health had worsened; diarrhoea compounded it. I bought medication from a local chemist, which ameliorated my condition to some extent.

We reached Gaurikund Government office where we could book horses and dolis. We secured one horsewala the moment we reached. Soon we booked horses for Jasmina, Bini, Kaka, Uncle and me. However there was shortage of dolis. One horsewala told us that we will have to book the dolis but we didn't know when we would get it. Hearing this, we tried to convince three of them to come on horses. However Mom protested. Kaka and Jasmina got angry with Mom, remembering the helicopter cancellation the previous day. We feared we would miss the darshan. Once bitten, twice shy. We assured her that she will be safe on horse and if she gathered courage to come on horse she would have good darshan. Lilaba and Aunty also wanted to avoid going on horses. Mom had taken a firm decision that if at all she had to go, she would do so by doli or else she would spend the night in a hotel in Gaurikund. Lilaba also seconded Mom's decision. Kaka and Jasmina got really annoyed. We knew that it will be difficult for them to go on horses but we were worried that they would miss the darshan. If they miss darshan today, who knows when Bholenath may call them again, which irritated Kaka and Jasmina more.

After hearing of Mom's firm decision, in anger we started climbing without wasting any more time. Aunty, despite undergoing an operation of the leg, was firm about having Bholenathji's darshan. We advised them to look for doliwalas. In case they did not get one, they should stay in a hotel nearby. We started off on the 14 km track. Roads here were broader than in Yamnotri. They had laid stones on the kachha road. I thought people had no reason to be afraid as the roads had a safety railing all the way. White tiny clouds were hugging the mountains gently. The snow clad mountains were shedding the snow. It was cold but we were enjoying the natural scenery, which was like a feast for our sore eyes. The sun seemed to turn cold due to the Himalayan cold. Though we could see the sun it was pleasant. The divine light of Shivji had subdued the powerful solar rays. The killer winds blowing from the snow-clad mountains chilled our bones. No pilgrim would bear even one night's chill if it were not for the attraction of Shivji's darshan. We went along looking at the small and nascent streams of waterfalls. I was listening to the chants of Om Namah Shivay on my Blackberry phone; the chants were reverberating around. In Himalayas' pure air, I felt as if I was meditating. It was quite a soothing experience.

The horsewalas were skilled and fast. We reached Kedarnath at around 1.45 pm. We tried vainly to contact Mom and Lilaba to know whether they could find a doli or whether they were coming for the Darshan, but to no avail. There was no network, nor could we contact from the horsewalas' phones. Horsewala dropped us at a particular place from where we had to walk around 1 km up to the temple. We started walking towards the temple, but Uncle was tired. He hired a pittuwala, due to which he could reach earlier. When we reached the temple premises, we saw him enjoying a plate of hot gulab jamun. He could not resist temptation, and feasted on hot gulab-jamuns even before the darshan. We were used to it, so we were not surprised. But we chided him for having them alone.

The moment we saw the temple we were amazed by its ancient architecture. The brick-red temple was supported by huge columns hemmed in by sky-scraper mountains from all sides, dwarfing us, making us think how insignificant we were. Time stood still here. We would just play a miniscule role on earth and leave ,without any signs to show of having lived. You would be left with nothing but your good karmas. Those who understood it, their egos dissolved. We got purified after taking a dip in Gangaji but even ego gets dissolved before the darshan.

It is a difficult proposition to build a temple nowadays. We wondered how Pandavas could have built the temple with limited resources 6,000 years ago! It was revived later by *Adi Sankaracharya.*

Thousands seek peace here and yearn for the darshan. Is peace possible? Your mind works overtime even in peace, preventing you from experiencing peace. We reached the temple in 20 minutes. We joined the long queue. Everyone was impatient to have darshan.

We could see the river behind the temple. A huge shamiana was raised to accommodate the surging pilgrims. The ringing of bells added to the spiritual ambience. We were not fortunate though; the temple would be closed between 3 and 5 pm, and the line halted. Uncle was impatient to come out; because of claustrophobia he could not stand here till clock to strike 5pm. We waited in queue for the 5pm. After 5pm Shringar Darshan preceded by Darshan of Abhishek.

Time moved slowly. While we were still standing in the queue waiting for our turn to come, black clouds gathered menacingly. The climate had suddenly changed. None of us realised the implication of this sudden change. Someone remarked aptly that the fashion in Mumbai and climate in Kedarnath change at a moment's notice. While we were still standing in line, the rains arrived. Thunder ricocheted after striking the mountains. The big droplets striking the stones sounded harsh in the calm atmosphere.

Even after 5.30 the temple doors did not open. Braving heavy rains devotees were still standing for the darshan. No one wanted to budge an inch.

In spite of facing hardships of icy rains and chilly weather, the devotees' ardent desire to seek the darshan of Shankarji became stronger. They wanted to blend in the hues of Shankarji. If this is not the power of Shankarji, then what is it? If this is not faith reposed by his devotees on him, then what is? Our legs were paining; we could not stand anymore. The body gave up against the cold. The whole body became numb like a log of wood.

Finally, after much shouting, the temple's doors were thrown open for the Shringar Darshan at 5.35 pm, accompanied by the blowing of a conch shell three times, electrifying the crowd. In the front we saw the statues of Nandi and in the sanctum sanctorum we saw Pandavas, Draupadiji, and Krishnaji. The ling was shaped like a buffalo's triangular hump as described in the Puranas. Shivji's calmness, grandeur and purity pervaded the atmosphere. I was feeling very blessed as I felt His presence. I felt as if I had been liberated from the cycle of birth and rebirth, I was disconnected from the world's thrall. I felt sublime. It washes the sins making you feel holy and innocent like a child beseeching his father (Shivji) for liberation. His darshan improves the lot of one's posterity. I was overwhelmed by the Darshan of Kedarnathji. I felt as if I had merged with Shivji. I had achieved equanimity; body and mind were like clean slate. There was a fusion between soul and the primordial self.

The picture continued. Heart and mind were strung by Shivji alone.

Soaked to the skin, we were collecting our shoes, when, to our utter surprise, we saw Mom coming towards us. I was so overjoyed to see her. I ran and hugged her tightly. We had been looking out for them. They got the dolis and came up. Seeing them we were much relieved. Mom told us that in Gaurikund they (Ba, Aunty, Mom) were struggling to find dolis. There were two windows for booking dolis. One of them was closed. Everybody queued up at the opened window; it was a long queue. Mom stood in the line, while Lilaba went ahead, exploring other possibilities. The line moved slowly. When the second window opened, luckily Lilaba saw it first and ran to stand first in the queue. They booked three dolis - one for each. All roads open up once you get an invitation from Shivji. If we had missed them, it would have been a tough task to search them as mobile network was not available. We would not have known whether they had got the dolis, whether they would find us as we had forfeited the Kanpur House's booking for yesterday. No wonder tears of relief welled up when we met them. Mom had managed to gather her self-confidence and will-power. After Mom we saw Lilaba and Aunty. We asked them to go for the Darshan. It was a great feeling that we all were together now.

Surreptitiously rain was playing out its part. We distributed work. Jasmina and I went in search of Kanpur House for checking availability for spending the night. PG Uncle and Kaka went to find out other possibilities of night stay. It started raining so heavily now that the whole Garhwal Mountain range was enveloped in a thick fog. We got wet completely and our legs froze. Due to extreme cold, Bini gave up and sat in second shop next to temple waiting for the three ladies to return from temple.

Fog was worsening visibility. We could not open our eyes because of the rain drops. Somehow passing through small by-lanes, we managed to locate Kanpur House where we had booked for the day before, which was cancelled as we were late by a day. We were in for a surprise when hotel manager spoke rudely when we requested for fresh bookings. He did not listen to reason. We decided to go back. Rain had increased its ferocity. By the time we returned, the lanes were flooded. Ankle-deep water numbed our limbs. With god's grace, Uncle found a small hotel for us to stay in. We gathered in the shop where Bini was waiting. The doliwala told us to come at the same shop the next morning at 6.30 am to leave for Gaurikund. We got divided in two groups - Kaka, Jasmina, Bini and I in one group and PG Uncle and three ladies in second group. As per Uncle's instruction. Gradually we started walking up the slope. After walking for a few minutes, as we (Kaka, Jasmina, Bini and I) looked back, to our chagrin the others had disappeared. It seemed we did not follow Uncle's instruction to Badri Palace; instead of taking the first left we went straight, thereby missing the hotel.

To our surprise, there were three hotels bearing the name Badri Palace. We visited them each, twice in an hour but could not locate the correct one, which was very frustrating and annoying. Kaka was very much tired and his body was unwilling to support him. We were clueless again. We decided to sit in the same shop from where we had separated. If they were searching for us we will be spotted.

We were waiting for the rain to stop and family to arrive, but neither seemed to be happening any time. A little later a young boy came running towards us, while taking deep breath he asked, "Patel...?" We nodded and he escorted us to the Dwarka Palace Hotel. By mistake Uncle gave us the wrong hotel name. Hearing this, without any second thought, we huddled in a room. The capacity was for four persons. Jasmina, Bini, Kaka and I settled in one room and the rest in another.

We had no strength to take off our shoes. We comforted ourselves with the blankets. Those were wet too. Not changing our positions for hours, we kept ourselves cocooned inside the wet blankets, sleeping closest to each other. The same boy came with the dinner which Uncle had arranged for. Nobody had the strength to get out of their blankets. Bini, Jasmina and I slept on empty stomach. It was freezing too much now. We could judge the intensity of rains by the heavy thundering and lightning as the night progressed. It was unstoppable. The hailstones were pounding on the roof, making a chattering sound. The lightning seemed to bounce between the mountains. The Mandakini was at its ferocious worst. Both the banks got inundated. We could hear all the sound and fury in the room. We were frightened and our morale was low too. As the night progressed we were more frightened. As if we were witnessing the Bhairav Roop Darshan. Shivji was performing the Tandav Nrutya making his group dance to his tunes. Residing with the group of ghost, Bhutafala was enacting the Natraja Darshan. The clouds joined in the fun, matching their steps in unison. We were shivering with fear caused by the sound and fury of the two matching their steps.

There was no respite from the rains. Bini and I were sleeping arm in arm to get more warmth. Kaka was not keeping well. Not for a second did we think of opening the window. He could not breathe properly because of the improper ventilation causing suffocation. He was feeling very uneasy. Kaka opened the door and started taking deep breaths. Seeing Kaka's condition, we could not sleep. We were anxious and clueless. As Uncle was carrying a cylinder of oxygen we thought of procuring it from him. We tried to open the door; because of heavy winds, rain water splashed into the room. Kaka and I called Uncle helplessly. Our shouts were not audible to him because of the heavy sounds of continuous hailstorms and cloud bursting. Rain was pouring like tap water in full flow. Helplessly and disappointedly we returned to our beds. Anger always follows loss.

I asked Kaka to sleep next to me as there was a window nearby so that he could inhale fresh air. My only concern was Kaka's health. The situation was very sensitive and difficult. It was a real war-like situation. It was fight against the unbearable cold and the aim was to return unscathed. This turned out to be my toughest tour ever. In times of adversity and misfortune, my Bholenathji would see us through.

Return from Kedarnath

June 16, 2013 DAY 12

We passed the night chanting Bholenathji's name. At four in the morning, we could see black clouds meandering menacingly, threatening to spew out destructive potion, shutting out the sunrays. It rained cataclysmically throughout the night. The falling rain water on the ice increased the cold, chilling us to our bones causing numbness and disorientation. As the cold increased, the clouds settled lower. We felt as if we were floating on the clouds. The black clouds got trapped in the mountain range as there was no space to move and crashed into each other causing cloud-burst and subsequent deluge. The Garhwal region experienced their fury and rage throughout the night.

It was now 5.30 am. Everyone got up feeling restless. We did not know which room the others were in, and waited for them to come out. When we did not see anybody coming, Kaka remarked, "I am going for the Darshan." We stared at him; what was he up to in such heavy rain as he was not keeping well! We advised him to wait till the rains subsided but to no avail. Jasmina also could not stop Kaka. Kaka was determined because of his immense faith, and said, "Do not worry, nothing will happen to me." Jasmina said, "Okay, I am coming with you." They left for the Temple. They had a good darshan. Due to rain and cold, only a few pilgrims and *pandas* had turned up for darshan so early. They were fortunate to enter the sanctum sanctorum today and had the darshan of Pandavas, Krishnaji and Draupadi. There was no sound other than the roar of Alaknanda and the ubiquitous rains. It was Shankarji and them; a rare darshan. Generally the *pandas* would not allow you to have more than a minute of darshan. They also heard the Shiv tandav stotram on his cell phone and returned satisfied.

While returning, Kaka sought advice from the same shop guy whether it was safe to leave since it was raining so heavily. He said it was a common phenomenon here; if you wait for the rain to stop then you may have to stay for days. He also informed Kaka that since you reached late, doliwalas, after waiting for some time, had left due to heavy rains.

On returning, he described enthusiastically the good darshan he had. I could not hold myself. Fighting cold and mustering courage, I also left for darshan and Bini joined me. I was ready for a special date with Mahadevji. I took dhoti, ghee and Gangajal along with me. Kedarnathji is so pure that nothing short of Gangajal will do for his Abhisekh. We had to wade through cold water. The moment I stepped in the chilly water, my feet became red like tomatoes and went numb. Any injury would go unnoticed; presently we reached the temple.

Luckily there were hardly five devotees, and the *panda*'s chants and mantras while performing the puja resonated. The moment we entered the sanctum sanctorum I felt spiritual satisfaction, equanimity and a rare calmness. We performed Abhishek with ghee, and it had to be squeezed out from the plastic bottle as it was frozen. I also offered dhoti and Gangajal. We prayed, "*Hei* Maheshwar, *Hei* Ashutosh, *Hei* Anantdrushtiwala, I am blessed by your rare darshan." All my wishes seemed worthless. "Shower blessings on your devotees." I did not feel the chill anymore; instead there was warmth, fulfilment and satisfaction. I had goose pimples while praying. My mind was engrossed completely, and the resulting vibes through my mind and body. The fluctuations of thoughts got streamlined. I felt as if I have attained a state of meditation. My mind attained a tranquil state by just entering the temple. Hence he is also known as Dhyandeep. I am short of words to express my state of mind at that time. We were feeling happy and blessed. The divine darshan of Mahadevji was heart-touching and overwhelming. His presence attracted me towards Him. It was difficult to leave. Bini and I returned from the temple satisfied.

A little later, Uncle and others came out of the next room to ours. We sighed in relief. Everybody had come out of their rooms to discuss the future course of action. We had called the doliwalas at 6.30 am but got late waiting for the rains to subside. Uncle ordered tea and biscuits. The same young boy who had escorted us the previous night brought it. We called him Chhotu. When we were fighting with the cold, Chhotu was helping everyone. Even in such a situation he was running around serving the pilgrims. He was honest and a good boy. I was impressed by his attitude and dedication towards his work. Kaka gave him money to buy biscuits for us. He brought biscuits and gave us the change. Presently he came back running and informed Kaka that he had given Rs 10 less and push a Rs 10 note towards him. Kaka was impressed with his honesty and so were we. Kaka asked him to keep the change and buy chocolates for himself. He was delighted and happy. Giving was a joy.

Our hotel also was getting inundated gradually. Mom, Ba, Uncle and Aunty were tired and fearful wondering how they would climb down. Given the choice, everyone would prefer to stay put. Bini was getting restless and impatient. She grimly said, "Ektaa we shall die of cold; do not want to stay here to die. Inform Kaka; let us go down." I kept consoling her and asked her to have faith in God. Kaka was keen to visit Badrinath. Further, as we were already late by a day, he did not want to delay further. It was raining incessantly for 10 hours with no sign of abating. Everybody agreed that it was senseless to stay back in the cold. It will be better if we go towards Gaurikund where the conditions would be less severe.

In the meantime, as we entered our room, a lady came rushing in the passage. She was scared and worried. She was accompanied by her mother who was sitting on a pittu fully wrapped in plastic to protect her from the rain. She removed the plastic, and we saw her mother was freezing. She was stiff and could not move even a single limb. It was terrible. We watched stupefied. The current situation had made us weaklings; even our minds were frozen. Thinking and questioning sensory organs gave in. The lady did not stop; she moved on.

Devotees are drawn to Shankarji and overcome ordeals because of their faith and devotion. Uncle and the three ladies wondered: *How will they go out in such a situation? How would we climb down though Rajnibhai was very determined to? Was it possible?* Questions were running through everyone's minds but nobody expressed them. Kaka was determined and informed us that we were leaving.

Without wasting a minute we donned our raincoats and started our journey. The next task was to find the doliwalas. We went to the pickup point, but could not find them. We thought of going to the booking office in search of them and make fresh bookings for everyone in case we did not find one. To reach the booking office we had to walk for at least a kilometre. Those who could walk (Kaka, Bini, Jasmina and I) began walking. Luckily, on the way, we found a pittuwala. We asked him to pick up the ladies from the hotel and bring them to the booking office. We did not know what Shivji had in store for us. The streets were deserted. Both sides of the road we could see small shops covered with black plastic sheets. The plastic sheet was also used for entering the shop. Not a soul could be seen.

The booking office was deserted. There was no sign of any doliwala or horsewala. Nothing was in place. In the whole hushed and tranquil Himalayan region, there were only black clouds looming large over snow topped mountains and us, nobody else. We fearfully walked forward looking on both sides of the road. Suddenly a gale blew away the plastic sheets exposing pilgrims and horses packed like sardines. We stood rooted, wide-eyed and stunned. When we looked back we saw four pittuwalas bringing the ladies with Uncle. For a fraction of a second, my heart stopped. We felt relieved and rejuvenated. We started lifting the plastic coverings of the shanties to check whether our doliwalas were taking shelter. We made five rounds but to no avail. Disheartened, we stood at a crossroad. We saw Uncle and Aunty relishing Maggie at a stall. We continued the search operation. Suddenly Bini espied Mom's doliwala; we ran towards him. We were overjoyed. We requested him to search for more doliwalas as otherwise we could not leave. Finally in a few moments we found them all!!! It was a great relief.

Now the task was to find horsewalas for ourselves. We enquired with a few horsewalas but they refused as no one wanted to risk the lives of their costly horses. We decided to walk. We wondered at our courage and perseverance to continue walking and who inspired us to proceed against all odds. Uncle reluctantly admitted that he could not walk and wanted a horse. I said, "Okay Uncle, let's start walking, and we will find them on the way." A little later, I saw one horsewala. "*Niche jaaoge*?" (Will you take us down?) He nodded. I let Uncle negotiate. We started moving ahead. Now we were four of us - Kaka, Bini, Jasmina and I - walking. Ashutoshji gives instant gratification to his devotees.

Of one thing we were sure - that it was not going to be easy, but we experienced courage coursing through our systems.

We came across a waterfall; the first of its kind. While going up it had been small and innocuous. The same waterfall had become a monster now. It was roaring like a lion and falling with unbelievable force. The gale was strong enough to sweep us off our feet. We stopped stupefied. Like us, many other pilgrims along with some foreign tourists were also standing in front of it. Everyone was clueless about what to do and how to navigate it. This rivulet coursed its way through the mountains.

Suddenly Mom's doliwala came running from behind and crossed a metal bridge supported by wooden planks. They thudded their way out. We mustered courage to cross the bridge. Forming a human chain and chanting Har Har Mahadev we scrambled and crossed it.

Mom's doliwala advised us to walk a bit away from the mountain and continue walking since it was raining. We were happy that we could cross the hurdle. It was too dangerous for us. Bini and I formed one pair and Kaka and Jasmina brought up the rear. We thought it must be the only hurdle we had to cross but soon we realised we were wrong. There was a huge landslide ahead of us. The road had shifted and was strewn with loose soil that turned sticky and was covered with roots and trunks of uprooted trees. Our morale was down by now and we were fearful. We could see the rivulet make its way through the mountains. We took small steps and held hands as we passed the stretch. We were unaware of what was in store for us. Anything could have happened now. In pairs we started walking fast along with the other pilgrims. We had no idea whatsoever about the extent of destruction that had been already wrought and how much more havoc was going to be wrought. Only thing we could do now was to go on walking. The rivulet had brought along the small and big stones with it. As big stones were displaced, roads got disintegrated. Regardless, we continued ignoring and overcoming any and all obstacles; marching ahead undeterred. One year to 75-year-olds were seen slogging through the difficult terrain. Many couples had carried their children on their shoulders. Some strapped their young ones snugly around them. Rain continued unabated and Mandakini River was flowing with increasing ferocity.

Many waterfalls, which were not even in existence the day before, had been formed. That was overnight evolution for us! We had to cross them all hand in hand.

After a while water level increased. Chilly water flowed over the sloppy and snaking roads. It was gushing through our legs with great force. Wading through the knee-deep water downstream on submerged sloppy roads needed us to push ourselves forward. We were zapped and our strength sapped. We were worried about the stones falling over us and the railings giving way. It was double whammy. There was no way but to remember Shivji and proceed further; come what may. We had to get out somehow. Dejection, depression and demoralisation were clearly evident on our faces. Still we all chugged along. Everyone was trying to survive, endure, outlast and protect against the vagaries of the nature. The climate was very chilling and we were wet to the bones. I was shivering like a leaf. Due to the pressure of water our legs were buckling. People slipped, fell down, but again they would get up and start walking fast so that they could get out. Who would guess how much more ferocious Mandakini would get? It was getting chillier by the minute as the clouds gathered, precipitating further cloud burst, increasing the intensity of the rains. The pressure was building up due to the cold.

Passing through many small and big waterfalls, we managed to reach Rambada at around 3pm, which is exactly half way between Kedarnath and Gaurikund. We could not believe we had actually walked 7 km in the worst possible conditions. We still did not see Mom, Lilaba or Aunty and did not know their whereabouts. As soon as we took a turn after a few shanties, we saw them waiting anxiously for our arrival. She was overjoyed to see us safe and sound. Bini and I reached first, followed by Kaka and Jasmina. Mom called out to me loudly. "I am here," I called out and ran to meet her. We all felt a big relief as we embraced.

It revitalised me. Mom is Mom. Mom is irreplaceable. I realised and felt that there is Heaven at her feet.

I could see a crowd of doliwalas and many stranded pilgrims there. All of them had occupied 30-35 black plastic covered shanties selling tea and Maggie, five to six government guest houses and a few shanties on first floor level. We entered a shanty for shelter from rains. All of them were pack to the rafters. There was no respite from the torrential rains.

Mom was very scared. Her doliwala refused to go ahead as there was a huge landslide and four of the other doliwalas were thrown off in the valley. Many pilgrims were buried in the rubble and dead. Our doliwala also gave us news of two other pilgrims who died due to landslide. They were walking past and were buried in the landslide rubble. They died on the spot. All doliwalas were anxious and nervous. They were discussing among themselves the next step to take. Meanwhile Uncle arrived royally riding his brown and tall horse as if a king was overseeing his subjects' welfare and well-being. No other horse could be seen carrying any passenger except Uncle's horse. We called him and he saw us. We were united again. Mom told me that she saw Lilaba and Aunty sitting in the opposite shanty.

The road was completely occupied by the doliwalas on both sides; there was no space to walk. People were still coming down. Everyone was trying to squeeze in the already cramped shanties. We were getting afraid and anxious.

Uncle too came inside the shanty and, as usual, ordered tea for himself first and then asked us. We did not want to have any as we had lost appetite due to fear. We just wanted to leave and reach the Gaurikund Valley. We halted there for around half an hour; I was sitting on the ground at the edge of the shanty taking the support of one of the dolis in the rain without feeling any of it. My head had gone numb by the too frequent falling of hailstones. Mom was sitting on the chair. Jasmina settled in a pittu. Even Bini got a chair to sit on. She removed the bag from her tired shoulders and kept it below her chair. Kaka stood behind us with Uncle, who was enjoying his cup of tea. A fair and heavy set young man from an adjacent shanty approached me, informing me that he was looking out for some place to stay overnight as the roads were blocked. I wondered why he should tell me about it. It seemed as if he was warning me of events to come; setting off a train of thoughts.

I looked at Kaka; he also heard him but did not express his thoughts. I told Kaka, "Let us go and find some place to stay. Roads are blocked and rains are not holding up at all." In fact, it had increased and water levels also rose alarmingly. I was frightened and could not fathom what I could do for my family. Where could I find a safe place for my family? Kaka's legs were paining; he did not feel like leaving the shanty and walk. He wanted to search for accommodation but the body refused to cooperate. I insisted he should do it all the same as everyone had already started reserving. Kaka gathered all his courage and we left the shanty in search of another place.

At no time did we think of giving up. We remained positive in spite of the insurmountable difficulties. Where did we acquire the positive thoughts from? We do not have to be afraid of any difficulties. There is always a way out; only, we need to find one.

Kaka reconnoitred the area of around 500 metres, where we saw some guest houses and a bigger version of shanty-like small houses. We inquired for some space, but as expected, everything was full. There was no space to keep a single foot even.

I felt people had been smarter in leaving Kedarnath earlier and lucky to have the space.

With disappointment writ large on our faces, we came back. Seeing our faces, Mom realised that we could not find a proper place. We asked one of the doliwalas to check the latest information about the landslide. He went but did not come back. Another doliwala offered to find out. I told him worriedly that your colleague had not returned yet; if you also do not come back...? He calmly replied, "*Madam, chinta mat karo. Hamaare do aadmi aapke saath rahenge. Woh aapko chhod ke kahin nahi jaayenge.*" (Madam, do not worry. Two of my men will be with you; they will not leave you in the lurch). We reluctantly said 'Okay'. In the meantime, locals dared to proceed further.

After some time, Mom's doliwala asked us to move ahead slowly.

While leaving the shanty, Bini got up looking for her blue colour bag. To her surprise, there was a black colour bag but not blue. The bag contained currency notes and other valuable things. Panicking, she told us about it. We looked around frantically and were disappointed when we could not find it even after a lot of search. Jasmina told her to take a chance and open the black bag. Fortunately that happened to be hers! Seeing her bag, Jasmina affectionately tapped Bini on her head for making all of us anxious. When she could not find her blue bag, she panicked and thought it had been stolen. We all laughed at her. Due to heavy rains the colour of the bag changed from blue to black.

We started walking. We hardly walked for 10 minutes when we met the first doliwala who had left earlier. He confirmed that what people were saying was true. There was a huge landslide ahead. We kept walking for some time.

Then we came across another shanty. Uncle quickly got inside it and ordered tea for himself. He was lucky to get a seat, and did not offer us any. The shanty owner would not allow us to enter because we had ordered only one cup of tea. He said, "*Wo jo kal raat se yahan baithe hai, wo bhi bahar nikalne ka naam nahi le rahe, ab tum bhi andar aaoge to hum kahan jaayenge? Nahi nahi, yahan nahi.*" *(*Those who are sitting since last night, are not willing to leave. Now if you too enter; where shall we go? No, no, not here*)* Sarcastically I said, "Ham nahi aayenge" (Okay, we won't enter.*)* I tried to relax on the staircase in full rain in a nearby shanty. Our doliwalas were observing. They asked us to leave the place and keep moving ahead. They were very supportive. We agreed to proceed.

As we were marching ahead, Uncle went to one of the shanties and returned with the news that he was giving us some space to stay and also offering us quilts and beds to sleep. We were in two minds. In the meantime, one of the doliwalas said, "*Aage rasta pura tuta hua hai aur khatarnaak hai. Yeh risky hai par hum aapko sambhal kar leke jaayenge.*"(The roads ahead are completely broken, it is dangerous and risky but we shall take you safely). Hearing this Lilaba's and Aunty's doliwalas started fighting with him. They were reluctant to proceed further. They were scared like us. They said. "*Hum lekar jaayenge per kuchh hua to hamari zimmedari nahi*" (We shall take them; however it will not be our responsibility if anything happenes). I asked Mom's doliwala, "Aap sambhal ke leke jaayenge na?" (Will you take us safely?) He said, "*Chinta mat karo madam, hamari zimmedari.*" (Do not worry madam; it's our responsibility).

Immediately we took the decision that we will move ahead as there was still time for sunset. Uncle was insisting on staying as his horsewala refused to go ahead because of the danger. As it is, Uncle's mind was seeking the warmth of the blankets in the shanty. However we decided to proceed further together. We recalled Trilokpati's name and moved forward. One good thing; while walking we noticed that the chilly rain water was not flowing over the road. After Rambada it got diverted and started flowing straight into the raging river, which was a relief as we did not have to wade through icy waters. However the rain-God was in his elements. It was pouring continuously accompanied by gusty winds. The Kalima was at her fiery best like we see in Hindi movies. The clouds had gathered due to her wrath. The earth seemingly quavered with tremors. There were landslides all around. Kalima caused destruction in her wake.

We walked to get night shelter. In spite of getting one, we had rejected it and decided to walk ahead. The roads were full of landslides making it dangerous to tread. Who gave us the inspiration to proceed further? While walking, we came across a number of broken dolis, damaged by the landslide, and uprooted trees were strewn all over the path. We were shocked to see the mayhem. Our hearts skipped a beat. We paused for some time at one of the accident spots. Doliwala shouted at us and urged us to move fast. The scene was horrible and terrible, beyond what words can describe. Doliwala helped us cross the area. We ran literally looking up in the fear of stones and boulders falling on us.

As we crossed hardly another kilometre, we saw a huge mountain caving in. It was a monster. This was worse than the earlier one. The mountains were swept by the monster waterfall. The scene was nothing less than a Hollywood action movie. The river caused landslide and started flowing over it. A big boulder blocked the road. Slime and sticky mud surrounded it. People were trying to circumvent it. People were shouting their family members' names and were cautioning them to be careful. They were screaming out of anxiety and fear. Families whose relatives were washed away were seen crying. Everyone was walking hand in hand with their family members. We were beseeching Palanhar for help. Heavy rains had made roads slippery and full of mud and slime.

One wrong step and you are gone. The condition had worsened. Many people slipped but managed to save their lives. Many of them were helping others to cross. A lady, who was walking just ahead of me, slipped and was helped by the man in front of her who held her hand and lifted her up. Bravo! Thanks to the young man. Now it was my turn. Thinking about the lady, my mind felt numb with fear. I lifted my first leg and was about to move the second when I slipped as the pebbles below shifted; time stopped still. My legs were in the air. I clung to the stones. I was perspiring in the cold weather! Eyes popped out and my energy was sapped. I pedalled, searching for some purchase. Kaka furiously screamed from behind. 'Ektaa...Ektaa...' For a minute I thought my game was up, but with God's grace, I was saved. Somehow I struggled and pulled myself up. It seemed that I was destined to live longer. Kaka admonished me, "Why can't you walk properly?" Adversity brings out the hidden courage in you.

Kaka was behind us. We helped a few others till Kaka came along. Keeping mom's doli down, her doliwala came running from behind to take us forward. As they reached, stones started coming down with greater force in front of Mom. We shouted loudly for Mom to be careful. We asked her not to stop and just keep moving forward. As she is obese she could not straighten up quickly. The mountain sides slid unexpectedly. We would have lost her if it had collapsed; just the thought made my hair stand and tears welled up. Broken dolis and buried bodies flashed through the mind. I urged her to continue in doli, come what may. We were on tenterhooks. Doliwalas warned us against talking loudly as the mountains being porous, they may tumble down any time due to slightest vibration. We may not have control over external factors but we can always control our thoughts. Think good and good things will happen. *Jo chaaho woh ho jaaye.* (Wish and it will be fulfilled.)

We started moving ahead. Again we came across another huge waterfall. They were increasing in size and speed. The whole scene resembled a video game created by God; we were clearing one level after another. With every level crossed, the game's difficulty level was increasing. The only thing different here was; we had only one life!!! One wrong move and you are finished. No second chance; no looking back, just pushing forward. One had to keep on walking irrespective of what was happening around you.

Mandakini was roaring with anger and swept anything and everything in its wake. There was another huge landslide. It had carried with it soil, pebbles, stones and uprooted the trees. Water was flowing furiously through them. Rivulets turned into waterfalls. Pilgrims were dead under the refuse and rubble. The humans who were called pilgrims earlier were now called 'bodies' and 'corpses'. There were plenty of them as a huge mountain had crashed down.

We could imagine what would have actually happened. It had created enough impact on us; physically and mentally. Our morale was broken. But we kept moving ahead; literally dragging our feet in spite of brain going blank at times. Another hill along with the road had been flushed in the valley. We had to overcome the white boulders. We saw many who lost their balance being washed away into oblivion. The flow and the whistling sound of the wind and the accompanying steady shower of pebbles were quite unnerving and daunting. Anyone could have been drawn in the vortex of water. Mom always warned us about three elements of creation, viz Air, Water and Fire. Today we got introduced to Water and Air. What a first-hand experience! Odds were heavily stacked against us. We were trying to overcome them one after another.

The road was full of pebbles and stones; even we could not make a track through it. One wrong foot disturbing the stones would qualify us as a candidate for Mandakini's lap.

I tried going through it first. The sound and flow of the waterfall was deafening. I passed through it safely and then offered my hand to Bini, followed by Kaka, Uncle and Jasmina. I was a little relaxed as all the three ladies were accompanied by their doliwalas, who were taking good care of them. Wherever slippery stretches were encountered, they treaded slowly. Credit to Mom's doliwala; he did not allow her to get down even once. Doliwalas of Lilaba and Aunty would help them walk through the muck and mud safely.

We trudged further. We saw there was hardly any remnant of about three quarter kilometre of a mountain. *Hei* Kailashnathji, *Hei* Kailashpatiji, how much more havoc are you going to cause? As there was total road blockage, pilgrims were stranded and were looking helpless. Many of them were helping each other. A young man was one of them. He stood exactly under the waterfall and helped many in crossing the waterfall. If God closes a door he opens another one. He was helping an obese lady. The lady was not able to balance herself against the flow of water. Suddenly her hand slipped and she was carried away by the water into the deep valley, tumbling down between the stones like a ball, and got trapped between the stones. In the flowing river we could see the pinkish tinge of her blood. This happened in a fraction of a second. Her family members were screaming for help. It was too late and obviously not possible to do anything. We were shell shocked; as if the picture on the TV screen had frozen. Heart beats slowed down due to fatigue. The shock triggered the beats again. More and more people gathered around and started helping each other.

Everyone stranded there, was scared of losing their dear ones. Now they had a firmer grip on the hands of their family members while crossing. Spectre of death was looming large on the horizon. The fear of being washed away or getting trapped and dying under debris of landslide was clearly visible on everyone's face. They were unaided and clueless.

Everything that was happening was unprecedented and unknown to the pilgrims. They wondered how much more Shivji would be testing their nerves and patience. Only Divya Drishti Shivji would know who was going to cross this ordeal. In just 15 minutes of death and destruction during which you can see your good and bad karmas streaming past your eyes just as Krishnaji showed Arjun during Mahabharat war. With God's grace somehow my family members and I safely crossed the waterfall.

We kept moving ahead slowly. After a while it was again the turn of a colossal landslide. It was considerably bigger than the last one. We could see it from almost 500 m away. We could hear booming sounds all around. We could not judge what would fall next, when and on whom. Reaching nearer we saw dead bodies strewn all over the place – it had become normal and usual for us by now. It was heart-rending. The bodies were smeared with mud. Some of the dead bodies bore signs of being hit by big stones. Hands and legs were detached from the body, getting trapped between stones. Some of them were too old while there were some children as well. One can hear the plaintive cries of the survivors. Many were buried in the rubble. Now the roads were muddy and slippery. The mud deposition was so heavy that there was an entire layer of it. I put my forward leg. I was horrified to see that I had sunk up to my knee. I lost my balance and fell. I tried again with the same result as I had weakened considerably. Bini, who was behind me, offered her hand. She lifted me up. I removed my shoes, cleared the mud and wore it again. I put my leg in again, and it got jammed inside. Again I removed my shoe and cleared it. One would think I was having a mud-bath! I had to repeat the same now and then. The whole stretch was strewn with dead bodies. Passing through and over them was disheartening and demoralising. It seemed that sympathy had taken a beating. Even the tears had dried up, and I was unable to express pain. It was the worst phase to be in.

We managed to cross two more landslides reaching 'Jungle Chatti', which was 3 kms away from Rambada towards Gaurikund. It was late evening and almost time for sunset now. Black clouds darkened the horizon even more. The rain was in full force. No, it had not stopped yet, which spelt gloom and doom for us. We could hear the sound of mountains crumbling in the Garhwal ranges. It added to the fear factor. Adding to it the constant lightening and thundering all around, which blinded us in the pitch darkness, almost every second and on all sides. While lightning was striking fear, the clouds were laughing, guffawing and cackling derisively. There seemed to be competition amongst them to see who was more frightening.

We saw around 10 shanties there. Among them three were on the hillside and seven on the edge of the road, facing the river side. They were typically loose structures made up of wood and supported by two bamboos, covered with black plastic on the edge of the road. Like in Rambada, stranded pilgrims had already occupied the entire space here as well. Looking at the crowd, myriad queries bombarded the mind: what is going to happen? Now what? Where would we stay at night?

The seven shanties were filled to the rafters. People in the shanties did not even try to move ahead and so were glued to their space, fearing losing their places. Many doliwalas were seen resting here. They were worried about their passengers as well as themselves. Pilgrims were a confused and fearful lot. They could not understand what was happening; why God was angry with them. There were many questions, but there were no easy answers. The roads were shortened due to the erosion of the edges. We thought people had gathered due to the imminent night. We could not see anything ahead. Due to heavy rains the street lighting was inoperative adding to the darkness as wires were seen dangling from the uprooted poles.

Doliwalas were discussing about one huge waterfall ahead which had broken the entire stretch of the road. We thought we can easily cross it as we had done many times before. But the huge crowd deterred our progress. It was not possible to cross it now and we would have to stay here till next morning. We asked one of our doliwalas to check the situation ahead. In the meantime Uncle came to Kaka and said, "Chalo Rajni bhai, we will have one cup of tea." We had to hand it to him. He kept his cool even in the worst situation.

In a few minutes, Doliwala came back running and said, that we cannot go ahead; we will have to stop. We all got upset hearing this; now how would we stay in such a pathetic condition? We stared at each other helplessly. Where shall we go in the pouring rains? We thought we were better off in Rambada. He said, "*Mere saath aao, kahi baithenge, chinta mat karo.*" (Come with me. We shall sit somewhere. Do not worry.) Bini started crying. We could see her tears in spite of the rains. There was no energy left. She was not in a position to utter a single word as we were freezing in the rain and cold. However her tears said it all. We had been walking under the open sky for more than 12 hours. In panic we told doliwala that as we had come this far, if we could reach Gaurikund, then there was nothing to worry. He said, "*Agar jaa sakte to main aapko le jaata na; upper se aa sakte thhe to main le aaya, per yahan se mumkeen hi nahin, agar pair bhi rakkha to niche jaayenge bahaav bahut zyada hain; meri baat maano."* (If it was feasible I would have taken you down. I brought you here as it was possible to come down from Rambada. But from here it is impossible; you cannot step in as the flow is furious. Listen to me). We felt helpless listening to the harsh truth. We were truly stranded as the road led to NOWHERE. We realised that Time is the most powerful. We cannot bring about things but Time can. Only Time can determine the course of events.

As we had to spend the night we had to take shelter in a shanty. However the rains were not in a mood to take rest. As we got near the shanties, we saw they were fully occupied by the pilgrims. There were around 50-60 people in each of them. Last in the line towards Kedarnath (from Gaurikund), there was some room in one shanty; I got a chair to sit. I called Mom, Bini and Jasmina so that we could settle there. Mom, Bini and Jasmine sat on the floor near me. Kaka and Uncle were standing outside. We got shelter inside the same shanty. Suddenly in the next 15-20 minutes, a group coming down from Rambada came to our place looking for shelter. In no time all shanties were over-occupied. Stranded people were directionless. As there was no place to move further, people started pushing into the shanties. As our shanty was the last in the row, it was getting filled slowly. Now even our shanty was brimming. There was not even place to stand. Many had to stand outside. It was even worse than Mumbai local trains in peak hours.

Lilaba and Aunty had managed to secure some place in one of the three shanties near the mountain side. The shanty was closed from all the sides, and it was getting difficult to breathe. People were standing outside as there was no space in any of the shanties. People surrendered themselves to God. Within half an hour our shanty owner came yelling at us. He was asking everyone to move out of his shanty as it was too weak to withstand the overload. He kept yelling at us, but due to heavy rain and landslide, his voice was inaudible. He was repeatedly shouting at everyone, "Baahar niklo zupdi tut jaayegi." (Come on. Get out. Shanty will collapse) His voice got drowned in the rain, lightning and the mountain crashing. *"Bahar niklo, yeh bahut kachha hain, mazboot nahin hain, yeh kabhi bhi gir sakta hain, sab mar jaayenge. Bhaago yaha se, bahar niklo"* (Get out. It is very fragile; not strong. It may collapse anytime. We shall all die. Scram from here; get out). Everyone was reluctant to move; they did not pay attention to him. Everyone was sitting, putting their faces down and avoiding to look at him. He got frustrated now; started pushing people off the shanty. He kept yelling on people to move out of it. "*Samajh me nahi aata tumhe? Baahar niklo, baahar niklo, sunaai nahi deta, gir jaayega ye?"* (Why don't you understand? Get out; can't you hear me? This will collapse!) He came to the person sitting next to me, held his hand and lifted him up, saying, *"Sunaai nahi deta hai kya...samajhta nahi tumhe?"* (Are you deaf? Don't you understand?) And he literally threw him out. He came to me and asked me to move out. As I was about to get up, Mom's doliwala came to my rescue and told him to leave us. "*Ye log hamare saath hai"* (they are our people). He left us alone but sent out another person who was sitting beside me.

Mom, Jasmina and Bini were sitting on a wooden floor when suddenly and shockingly they felt some vibrations. Fearfully Bini asked us, "Did you feel anything?" Jasmina tried to feel and said, "No." Bini had felt it; she was unconvinced with her reply. She knew something had happened and something more could happen. Again after another five minutes they felt another reverberation. But this time it was stronger. Both of them shouted for me to leave the shanty. "It is not going to hold up," they said. I pulled up Mom with me and ran out of the shanty. As we turned left, we heard another loud sound unexpectedly exactly behind us. It was probably louder than a bomb blast. There were huge and uninterrupted landslides occurring in the mountains behind us. We were just looking up wondering when the top will crash on us. Big and enormous rocks and boulders were rolling down swiftly. We were scared to look back. When we did look back, what did we see? It was a huge landslide that pulled down the shanty we were in. Phew!!! The shanty, within a fraction of a second, tumbled over and submerged in the raging river. We were mortified. As it was dark we did not see who fell down. That scene was so painful and frightening that it touched us deeply. It was just a matter of few seconds; otherwise we would have met the same fate. I could feel smoky inside even in this cold! Mind went blank. Heart beats were racing. My heart was in my mouth. Where are we? What are we doing? Why are we doing? Where are we going? There were many questions. No answers.

The vibrations were a clear indication to us that further catastrophe was on the cards and to those sitting inside to move out. Those who understood were saved. Those who did not, were now martyrs. God offers enough indications at every step. Depending on the road you choose, he allots the appropriate fruit. Instead of cursing God, it is better to rue your decisions. God after performing his duties leaves you to your fate. The incidents are pre-ordained but the degree of difficulty depends on the good karmas done by you. We thanked God for his warning signals and tried to console ourselves.

Shivji was showing his true colours of Rudra Swarup by performing the Tandav Nrutya. It was pitch dark. We had to judge the source of the falling stones from its sound. Mandakini was in her wildest mood. Electricity supply was totally disrupted. The sound of swiftly flowing river was the scariest. Hair stood on ends. We could not grasp the situation or its consequences thereof. What was happening around us? We had no strength to question God. We were unaware whether we would be living after a second. The elements were at their worst. We had no option but to wait.

We moved ahead in total darkness. We stopped in the middle of nowhere, not knowing where to go, as if on crossroads. At one end, the huts were toppling, and at the other end, the mountains were giving way. There was another shanty, adjacent to our old shanty. We had left our fate to God so we were a bit relieved! We were ready to be swayed by his push and pulls.

It was already over-packed. One could not see who was around you. The continuous damp head had numbed the brain activity. Knees were buckling due to weakness. The body was screaming to sit down. We dared to enter the hut knowing too well that the adjacent hut had just been washed away.

I got a place between two rows of chairs. There was hardly any place to stand. My legs were paining terribly; body was tired, mind totally blank and heart scared. Only thing on my mind - I have to be strong for my family. I squeezed myself and made some space to sit on the floor. After a while I made some space for Jasmina. I had adjusted myself by stretching under the chair, keeping my leg on her leg and feeling relaxed. I made some space for Bini. She got support for her back too. We were constantly moving our feet to be more comfortable. I was not able to bear my own weight. There was a person sitting behind me. I supported my back by placing a bag on his leg and leaning backward. He did not seem to mind. He did not object. After sometime my conscience made me realise that he too may be tired. The weight could be making it cumbersome for him. I tried to shift my bag and straighten up. He remarked, "*Nahi nahi, koi problem nahi hai beta aaram se baitho.*"(No, no there is no problem. Relax.) Still I could not do so.

We were surrounded by people. People were still trying to force their way in. Mandakini was ruthlessly flowing furiously, taking along with her all that came in her grasp.

The person behind me asked the shantywalla to give three to four packets of biscuits as he was hungry. As hotelwala could not find his way to us he passed on the biscuits and change via the people. He offered me two biscuits. I had not eaten anything for the last two days and I was tempted to accept it but my inner self did not allow me to take it. I didn't know how long he had been hungry, and I could not deprive him. I politely refused but he persisted. I felt guilty as my family was hungry, how can I have it alone? I said to him, "*Nahi nahi...thank you...aap khaalo.*" *(*No, no thank you, you have it.*)*

He then told me not to sit down but to squat. I could not comprehend. I looked at Jasmina; she looked back at me. We were silent and ignored him at first. After five minutes he again advised me. "*Madam khade khade baitho...agar bhaagna pada to turant bhaag sakoge.*" (Madame sit in such a way that you can run in emergency.) Now we understood, what he meant. We had already witnessed one big landslide earlier. We realised that we needed to be on our toes; should anything happen we should be in a position to run quickly. Meanwhile a lady came hurriedly and stamped on Bini so hard that she moved back and lost her place. The stranger had done it on purpose so she could get a place. Mom scolded her; how dare she do that! She pretended to be deaf. People were fatigued as they were on their feet for days and nights on end. They were directionless due to havoc wrought by Shivji.

As we stood up two doliwalas came and took our seats. Jasmina and I thought this must be their game plan to make us stand so that they can occupy our seats. We asked them to vacate our seats but they kept their heads down and did not listen to us. One man from behind asked them to get up quickly and vacate the seats. They got up and we regained our place. As we were about to settle down, we heard stones rolling from the mountains. This time it was bigger than the last one. We were scared. The sound left us paralysed. The man standing behind me told me, "The moment I say run; run immediately." I replied,

"Run where? There are landslides everywhere. How do I know where it is happening this time as I can't see anything." He pointed to our left and said, "Run this way." I said okay. Again we heard the loud sound of stones rolling down. He held my hand and pulled me out of the shanty. In the same way I held Bini's hand and ran out. It was now risky to stay inside. People who were standing jumped outside forcing us to come in front. We all stood in front of the shanty. Presently the stones stopped falling. People started going inside and settled themselves. Silence prevailed all round.

Jasmina, Bini, Mom and Kaka sat by edge of the shanty in a row. Uncle fitted himself in a doli in the middle of the way in the open, holding open an abandoned, broken umbrella. Someone pointed out that if anything were to fall on him, then it would be difficult to get up. He immediately got up and joined us.

A little later we heard a louder sound of land sliding shaking the ground. Everyone panicked and started running here and there in the dark. We could not make out if the mountains were falling or the shanties. As if competing in a hurdle race, everyone tried to come out of the shanty. People, who were standing behind Jasmina and Bini, started jumping over them. In the process one of their legs hit Jasmina and Bini hard on their shoulder. Both of them fell on the ground face down and Jasmina hurt her chin. She started shouting, "Kaka...Kaka...I'm dying." The person who still held my hand and I ran towards her. We pulled her out of the stampede. In the same way someone rescued Bini also. Anxiously we pushed the people back to search for Kaka as he had been sitting with Jasmina and Bini. Thinking the worst, we started clearing the ground. Jasmina called out, "Kaka where are you?" Kaka heard Jasmina's call and came to us, but he was forcefully pushed back to the original spot. She hugged Kaka in relief. Jasmina's chin was bleeding and because of rain it started dropping. We decided not to take the risk and stood in the middle of the road. People were trying to assemble their relatives by calling out their names. Rain was doing its job and Mandakini was not far behind. Landslide had occurred on the shanty adjacent to ours. We could not see it clearly but the loud reverberating sounds had impacted our minds greatly. People were shouting for help. Rains were not stopping at all but fell with the same ferocity.

Standing in the rains for hours on end made me shiver. My body was not able to bear the cold now. A stranger was holding me by the shoulder. I was shivering too much. He tried to find me a warm place. The shanties were filled to the brim. We got a space between the shanties covered by plastic sheet. He went inside and ensured that it can take our weights by tapping the plywood with his feet. First he checked by himself, then Bini and I joined. Jasmina also managed to squeeze in next to Bini. Mom and Kaka did not get space; so they stood outside in the rain. He told me to sit but I did not.

I: *Doliwale ho kya?* (Are you a doliwala?) He did not reply, maybe he could not hear.

I: *Doliwale ho kya? (Are you a doliwala?)*

Doliwala: *Haa, par pehli baar aaya hu; dosto ke kehne par, aur phans gaye.* (Yep, but I have come here for the first time on the advice of my friends; I am stuck.*)*

I: *Kahan se aaye ho?* (Where have you come from?)

Doliwala: *Kashmir. Aap kaha se ho?* (How about you?)

I: *Mumbai.*

People had no space to even stand due to the roads being washed off, forcing them to climb the mountains with torches; the glow helped us to monitor stones tumbling our way.

Meanwhile Bini realised something was crawling around her feet. She looked down and saw that we were standing on a plastic covered blanket generally used by the doliwalas to cover their wooden doli. It was swarming with earthworms. They were double the size of those found in Mumbai. She immediately ran out. I asked her, "What happened?" She replied with fear writ large on her face, "Look below." When I saw even I came out swiftly. The Kashmiri doliwala pacified me saying, "Nothing will happen, do not worry, they do not do any harm."

I stood with Jasmina. She suspiciously enquired, "Why was he helping you? You do not know each other; what is he up to? Is he taking undue advantage? Did he touch you inappropriately?" I said, nothing of the sort; he was not up to anything. He just held me by my shoulder. She advised me to take care of myself.

Kashmiri Doliwala said, "*Aapko bahut thand lag rahi hain, thhehro mai aapke liye chaai leke aata hu*' (You are feeling cold; let me bring a cup of tea for you). "*Nahi, theek hai, chalega,*" (Do not worry.) He would not listen; he brought a cup of tea for me. "*Mai akeli kaise piu; mere parivar ne kuchh khaaya piya nahi hain...*"(How can I have it alone when my family is hungry and thirsty?) This time around he provided everybody with a cup of tea. Jasmina, Bini and I went to Kaka and we all had a cup of tea. We all blessed the Kashmiri doliwala. In spite of having money we were poorer compared to Kashmiri doliwala today. If you think everybody around you is good, God will send only good people to you.

We waited there for some time. The Kashmiri doliwala took me to a shanty. He told me to wait outside. He gradually eased me inside the shop. I had held Jasmina who held Bini. Due to the weight the benches were breaking; we started hearing cracking sounds as the benches threatened to give way. People were not leaving their places. Time seemed to stand still. Every second was unbearable.

All were caught in the web of darkness; were waiting for the first ray of sunlight. A man was standing inside the shanty with his family. Rain was falling slant. He was holding an open umbrella at an angle to avoid the rain, and gave us some protection. We thanked him. We waited for two hours. I felt giddy as I was still feverish, and due to the tension and struggle, was fatigued. I was feeling dehydrated. My head had started spinning.

I asked doliwala to bring one packet of biscuit or else I will faint. He quickly went running and brought one ParleG. I had just a biscuit out of the packet and kept the rest for others. I offered him money but he refused to take the money. After sometime, he got a place to sit on a broken bench. He settled down there. Everyone was helplessly waiting for the first ray of dawn.

It was time for dawn. Now every second seemed like an hour. Time was not passing by; as if the clock had stopped ticking. We were all sitting helplessly without food and water. Rain was not ready to stop. We were soggy and muddy. It was probably the longest day and night of my life, and the scariest ever.

Suddenly one man came running towards Kashmiri doliwala. He was his friend. He told him, "*Chal jaayenge.*" (Let's go) I asked him promptly, "*Kaha jaaoge?*" (Where will you go?) He said, "*Madam hum sab saath me hai...jungle ke raaste se nikal jaayenge.*" (Madam we are together; we shall take the jungle route.) Before I could think of saying anything he disappeared. He was like an angel sent by Anant Drishti to help us, direct us and save us before vanishing in thin air.

Trilokpati facilitated the journey of Trilok. Today was Mom's birthday. Digambar was not ready to show his face through the black clouds. Rains were performing their show. Every scene was like the first and the last show. Every moment was important and memorable, etched in our lives.

DOHAS

Man feels he has done it,
But the doer is other one.
Work will remain incomplete,
If God wishes, shall be done.

Jungle Chatti

JUNE 17, 2013 DAY 13

The moment finally arrived for which we were waiting with bated breath; the first rays of sun peeped so we could see the mayhem wrought by nature in the daylight. People started trekking ahead. There was perceptible decrease in the number of people. One young group checked and found no change and came back and decided to go through the mountain route. Activity increased visibly. Many who went in the hope of leaving this place fast realised that there was no change in the force of the waterfall and trudged back. The sky took on a saffron hue.

Jasmina and I finally got a chance to rest on a broken bench. Mom and Kaka were sitting on a bench opposite mine. They were under a broken umbrella braving continuous rains. He did not betray any emotions. Without blinking he sat exhausted, defeated and fearful. Kaka was looking more restless than tired. He was feeling guilty that he could not do anything for his family. Considering his condition my struggle and efforts increased. I had not imagined that the feeling of helplessness was the worst feeling. He sat quiet most of the time. Looking at him I was feeling sad. I have never seen Kaka looking so helpless. I could not help crying. It was now more than 48 hours that we had not slept. Bini was restless and feeling very sleepy; she went to Mom and rested on her shoulder. At times you spent sleepless nights in the most luxurious mattresses but Bini could sleep even in a standing position! No amenities are enough for some people.

In such a heavy rain we wondered where people were heading and which route were they opting for in spite of the waterfall being very intense. Jasmina and I ventured out. I was witnessing the most horrible natural calamity we had ever seen in our lives. Last night a mountain had crumbled over our shanty in front of us, a rivulet cascaded into a waterfall. It brought along with it all the trees, stones, huge boulders and the usual muck in a free fall. Ultimately the mountain gave way and got swept into the valley in the blink of an eye. There were 5-6 such rivulets threatening to turn into monster waterfalls. There were booming sounds all around. We would be easily wiped out if a similar incident happened on our mountain. When man fiddles and messes around with the environment, nature may not react immediately but when it does, the form of destruction affects man severely and comprehensively by destroying life and property. People selfishly construct houses and buildings on river banks without assessing the consequences to the ecology, just so they can earn money. This played a big role in the scale of destruction and loss to human life due to the cloud burst.

I felt as if the opposite mountains had taken the Rudra Swaroop of Shivji. Every boulder, stone, pebble and particle that had fallen during the landslide seemed to disintegrate from his body causing unbearable pain. He also feels the pain due to the disintegration of his body. Humans are part of Him. Devotees' pain doubly affects Shivji. God is Avyayprabhu and Avinashi. Bhudev was experiencing pain at every tremor though it was pre-ordained and established by the Fate; there was no escape. Shivji (Anant Drishti-Perennial Visionary) was aware of the calamity but helpless due to Karma committed by us.

At about 7 am we saw a policeman running about. It seems he was posted in the police station located on the hill. Mom and Kaka were sitting next to the steps leading to the police station. He was alone and running here and there, very busy replying to queries. We approached him to seek help and guidance. We enquired about the future course of action we needed to take; what we can do and where we could go. He was tensed, was reluctant to give the answers. May be he was worried about his own life! Jasmina started walking with him and fortunately he gave some important inputs and clues.

Jasmina: *Ab ham kya kar sakte hai?* (What should we do now?)

Policeman: *Ye jagah per se jald se jald niklo. Yahan rehna khatro se khaali nahi hai. Kal barsaat me Rambada pura khatam ho gaya. Jald se jald jungle ke raaste se bhaag lo.* (Leave the place immediately. This place is dangerous. Yesterday Rambada was completely washed out. Immediately go through the jungle route.)

Jasmina stood rooted to the ground. The policeman called her, and she ran towards him.

Policeman: *Ek dukan bhi bachi nahi hai. Aur jinhone Rambada me aasra liya thha woh sab paani mein beh gaye. Ab yeh jagah ki baari hain. Kyu ki baarish bandh nahi ho rahi. Agle 24 ghante mein baarish ki agaahi huyi hai. Isiliye jald se jald yahan se niklo.* (Not a single shop was saved. Those who had taken shelter in Rambada were swept away. Now it is the turn of this place. Further, the rains are not stopping. Heavy rains are forecasted for the next 24 hours. That's why leave the place quickly.)

Hearing this we were dumbstruck.

I felt giddy; my mind was paralysed. I was totally blank. Standing between the mountains I felt dizzy. Sight blurred. Could not believe Rambada was no more. We were cursing ourselves for leaving Rambada yesterday where all facilities were available, including food. We couldn't believe the news! Who inspired us to leave Rambada in spite of all the facilities? We saw each other and breathed easy. Our belief in God strengthened; every second he was helping us.

Jasmina kept pace with the policeman silently. Policeman waited as someone called him. But without noticing, she walked ahead. Bini hailed Jasmina when she saw her walking alone. As there was no reply she called her again. Jasmina realised that Bini was calling. The policeman was still talking to someone. She ran after the policeman and asked him about the condition of the road. She explained that we were accompanied by three ladies. Was the road suitable for them? He said, *"Jaan bachaana hai to jaao, mein to bhaag raha hu."* (If you want to save your lives, leave. I am running.) Jasmina explained to him about Aunty's condition. He responded "A*ap chalo mere saath, mein sambhaal ke leke jaaunga."* (You come with me. I will take care.*)* We decided to leave.

Back in Kedarnath, a huge boulder hurtling through the Chorabari Talav stopping just short of the Temple. The flow of Mandakini swept along with the rain and Chorabari Talav water, carrying anything and everything in its wake. Fortunately Talav water circumvented the Temple. How come the Temple and its periphery were saved? This is nothing short of miracle. Shivji had immense, limitless and immeasurable Power which cannot be fathomed or understood.

Doliwalas of Aunty and Lilaba had to be relieved as they insisted that their dues be settled. However Mom's doliwala was with us. Jasmina came running and informed us that the policeman was ready to help and guide us further; let us start walking ahead. But everyone was reluctant to go. They wondered: How can we go through the jungle route? Jasmina and I explained to them the entire situation again and asked them to be courageous and move ahead as the place had become more dangerous now. If we wanted to live then getting away from this place was the only option. Finally, after some more coaxing, they agreed. The doliwala said, *"Madam aap log nahi ja sakte."* (Madam you people cannot venture ahead). But we vehemently said, "*Nahi ham koshish karenge, ham jaayenge.*" (We will try all the same.) He again told us, "*Mein abhi jaake aaya, aap log nahi jaa sakoge.*" (I just went and saw ; you all will not be able to make it.) As he was very well versed with the situation, he was right in discouraging us. However we thought we should give it a try. The rest of their team members were very much annoyed and wanted to leave to save their lives. Out of all only one doliwala did not want to abandon us, forcing others to be with us. He said, "*Aap mere saath aao...mein ab aapko utha to nahi paaunga lekin aapka haath pakad ke pahaad chadhne me madad karunga.*" (You come with me. I will not be able to lift you but I can help you to climb the mountains by holding your hand). We said okay. That was fine with us.

In the meantime a man fully smeared in mud came running. He was crying for help. His family was trapped in the landslide. He asked the officer for help. The policeman expressed his helplessness to do anything now as he had his own family to look after. He asked him to look for help elsewhere. We feared as rains may still continue there may be another landslide. Even if we wanted to help, we had a fear that we may get trapped in mud and muck. We all felt very sorry for the man. His family was dying in front of him; he could not do anything for them. There could not have been a more pathetic situation than seeing your family die in front of your eyes.

We started walking hand in hand in the direction of the jungle. Immediately we saw that tree trunks had occupied the entire road and had even destroyed it marginally. There were layers of mud and muck. We could not even go beneath the trunk; we had to go through the branches and roots.

Along with the tree a mountain also fell across the road. There were thick layers of mud and muck. It became more slippery and slithery as many people passed through it. It made walking treacherous. I tried to venture first. The moment I put my foot down I slipped. I did not fall completely as I immediately supported myself with my hand. Holding the tree I walked on the trunk. After crossing to the other side, I made Mom sit on the trunk. Due to their age and weight, it was an impossible task to expect the three ladies to manage the crossing. We had to cross the dead bodies buried underneath. We had to actually jump over the fallen trunk and branches. We somehow managed to cross it treading on the buried dead bodies.

Eventually,we reached a point from where the jungle path started. It was very slippery and fully covered with many trees. As we moved ahead there was a stable without roof. The wind had blown off the roof exposing the stable, which was fully packed with a group of aged people. They were shivering helplessly; their condition was precarious and pitiable. Their bony bodies were ridden with sores. We had to pass through them. The edge of the jungle was looming above at a 60 degree; an angle close to the vertical. We had to climb the steep incline which was filled with mud and dense trees. Just to cross 500 metres the policeman showed us a 14 km jungle route! We had to climb over the source of the waterfall and then climb down. We decided that none of us could do it. We aborted the plan summarily. Mom scolded us that in spite of their protests we were trying to make them climb. Doliwala also rubbed it in, "*Maine kaha thha na aap nahi ja sakte to bhi aap sunte nahin thhe!*" (I told you so; you cannot make it but you would not listen). Jasmina and I tried to pacify Mom.

We returned to Jungle Chatti crossing all hurdles all over again. As we reached,

doliwala said, "*Ab aap jungle ke raaste se nahi ja sakte to ab hame jaane ki chhutti do.*" (Since you cannot go by the jungle route, please relieve me.) Jasmina got scared.

Jasmina (raised voice): *Aap chhod ke jaaoge to hamara kya hoga? Yahan pe log mar rahe hain aur aap hame chhod ke jaa rahe hain? Mai apni aankho ke saamne apne gharwalo ko marte dekh nahi sakti!* (What will happen to us if you abandon us! Here people are dying and you are leaving us! I cannot see my family dying in front of my eyes!)

Her eyes and face turned red; she could not hold back her tears. He understood our predicament and replied:

"Madam zindagi ka sawaal hain magar mai aapko vaada karta hu agar kal sab salamat raha aur raasta khul gaye to subah jaldi aapko yaha per hi lene aaunga. Aur aap yehi dukan me baithe, yaha ki sabse suraksheet jagah hain. Agar kuchh bhi ho jaaye yaha se bahar mat aana; kitni bhi baadh aaye aap andar surakhsheet rahenge." (It is a question of our life but I promise that if roads get cleared, I will come here to pick you up in the morning. Stay put in this shop, which is the safest place. Do not leave the place under any circumstances. Even in the event of floods you will remain safe.) He pointed towards one of the shops from the mountain side where aunty and Lilaba had been sitting the whole night.

Before he completed his sentence I ran towards the shanty made up of blank plastic sheet. I lifted the plastic to get in the shanty. I saw three couples had already occupied the entire space. As I tried to open the plastic cover, one of the men yelled at me, "*Nahi...yaha sirf hum rahenge.*" (No! Only we will stay here!)

I felt nervous and pleaded with him for some place.

I: *Uncle puri raat ham bahar baarish me khade thhe. Aap hi ki tarah mere saath mera pura parivar hai. Pure bheeg gaye hain aur badan me taaqat bhi nahi rahi hain. Aise samay me ek insaan hi insaan ki madad nahi karega to kaun karega?* (Uncle we have been standing in the rain all night. Like you, we also have our family with us. We are soaked to our bones and are weak. Who else but a man can help a man in such trying circumstances?)

Man: *nahi nahi andar nahi.* (No. Not inside.)

Second Man: *Ha theek hain. Wahan wo kone me jagah hai. Wahan pe baith jaao.* (Okay. You can take the corner.)

Uncle behaved as if the entire place belonged to him. The shanty did not belong to him still I patiently explained to him. The shanty was very small. Benches were arranged as if a stage had been built on which six couples were sleeping in beddings. On the right next to the gate, there was a slope covered with plastic on which we were told to sit. I went out and called everyone. All of them were trying to get settled in the scant space allotted. Kaka and I were still standing. To find out some alternative for Kaka and me, I lifted the plastic. To my amazement I saw a buffalo in the middle of the road. I stood stupefied for a moment. How come a buffalo of all the animals! An idea flashed in my mind, whether Bholenathji was giving me darshan in the form of a buffalo as he had appeared before the Pandavas. I wondered how a buffalo could appear miraculously out of the blue. I went running towards the buffalo, touched it and bowed my head. It was a good omen. I felt unusually courageous, my faith in Shivji increased. He is with us all the time guiding us through difficult times.

While returning towards the shanty I saw a chair lying; it turned out to be broken. I threw it away. In the opposite shanty I saw one chair. I went running towards shanty and requested the owner to lend me the chair. He complained that people had broken all his belongings and there was nothing left anymore. I still insisted and guaranteed that I will return it in the morning. Finally he agreed. I kept the chair at the entrance and asked Kaka to sit on it.

When I retold the incident of the buffalo, he expressed surprise. He immediately lifted the plastic covering; the buffalo was nowhere to be seen. I was scared to sit at one place inside the shanty as last night I had witnessed many sudden landslides. I went out and started walking to and fro with an eye towards the mountains. I saw another horrific scene of dilapidated shanties and broken dolis scattered everywhere. It was still raining with the same ferocity and it was very windy too. Black evil clouds hovered over the mountains and over us. Innumerable rivulets had erupted from mountains. It was a horrifying view. We had to take shelter inside. I settled on one aluminium trunk case. Uncle and Aunty were in an adjacent shanty.

We just hoped for the rain to stop or weaken. We did not have drinking water or food. People who occupied the shanty before us were well equipped with shawls. We were freezing in the cold and rain. The plastic behind which we were sitting was torn, giving way to a freezing gust blowing inside with a clicking sound. To make matters worse, rainwater fell inside continuously, making the place wet. We were shivering. Empty stomach made us very weak. I was not able to withstand the cold. Once I felt I should go back to the place where we had found the earthworms and bring the blankets, but Bini asked me to exercise restraint. Aunty had found one chair and was relaxing on it while Uncle was standing next to her.

Lilaba and Mom pleaded with the other occupants to share some of their blankets or shawls with the girls as we were fully wet and dying of cold. They did not heed or help us at all. We put up a brave front as there was no other option. In the shanty a box of mineral water was lying in the corner next to me. I asked Mom if we could have it. Mom forbade me as the shanty owner was not there and we had to have his permission and pay him before having it.

It was so dark inside the shanty that even during day time we could not see each other's faces. The only task was to keep silent and listen to the sounds of falling raindrops on plastic of the shanty roof, estimate the severity of the rains and request Bholenathji to stop or reduce the rains. In the meantime, one of the men started vomiting inside the shanty. It was very nauseating and unbearable.

A lady enquired whether we have an unmarried girl in our midst. When I told her I was one, she gave me a bottle of Gangajal. We performed a ritual where I allowed the water to fall continuously amidst chanting of Mataji's shlokas praying for the rain to stop.

Sitting in the gloomy shanty at night thinking of the days gone by, a thought knocked the door of the mind: I was wondering how we were not scared in spite of travelling thus far. At every stage we were encouraged to have faith. I was feeling a vibration. At no stage were we stressed by any negative thoughts of whether we would return unscathed from here.

From where did I get the vibrations? I could get only one answer.

'Our strong steadfast and unshakable faith.'

I strongly believed that Kaka's praying to Bholenathji, and Aunty's and my abiding and enduring faith would help us come out triumphantly.

Around 6 pm the rain had reduced and finally by 8 it had stopped. Uncle came out of his shanty in search of food and called Kaka. He asked us about food, but as we did not want to have anything, we said no. Both of them went out, and when they did not return for a long time, we got worried. I called out to Aunty from my shanty and enquired about them. They had not returned yet. I started running in their direction calling their names. At last Uncle replied with, "*Khichdi saari hati.*" (Khichadi is good.) Uncle had convinced the shanty owner to give him place to sleep. He asked Kaka whether he wanted to sleep in the shanty. We were scared as it was located exactly on the end point of a curve. We dissuaded Kaka and asked him to be with us and also requested Uncle to be awake as it was risky to sleep.

We had to spend the whole night there. Bholenathji had heard our request and the rain had stopped. We relaxed a bit. It was obvious that no one could sleep though everyone had closed their eyes. It was a frightening day. Even the slightest sound would alert us. The whole day was spent in anxiety. Even now I wonder how we could have spent days and nights in the shanty when it was a difficult proposition to spend a day even in luxury. We did not realise then but dreams had become scarce. It was always a nightmare!

We were cut off from the outside world. Our relatives were not aware of our condition.. May be it will be broadcasted today. All whose relatives were in Kedarnath would be scared; praying for their early arrival.

Towards Gaurikund

June 18, 2013 DAY 14

The morning was very quiet but there was no change in Mandakini's flow. The damage had already been wrought overnight. There was an eerie silence that followed the mayhem. People were awe-struck. I came out of the shanty along with Bini. We got a complete panoramic view of the destruction, ruins and wreckage. The calamity was stupendous. Bini and I wondered whether the waterfall had reduced by now or not. We breathed a sigh of relief as we saw the flow had reduced substantially. Uncle came out of his shop and went straight to the opposite shop. He ordered tea and Maggie for everyone for breakfast. Suddenly it started raining again. We hurriedly finished our breakfast.

The rain had started and obviously could have led to the waterfalls swelling. Fearing that we will have to spend the night in the gloomy shanty, we decided to start moving immediately. There was frenzy and furore in the groups stranded as everybody decided to leave. The old and weak were apprehensive as they could not walk and all doliwalas had left. We did not want to be left alone. Nobody had the strength to lift the old and weak. It was obvious that Mom, Lilaba and Aunty had to walk out the remaining stretch. Mom and Lilaba agreed, but Aunty disagreed due to the leg operation and pain. She explained that it was not possible for her to walk. We started search for a pittuwala for her, but unfortunately we could not find one. After searching for some time, we decided to walk slowly. Mom and I started walking ahead together. Jasmina, Bini and Lilaba were together, while Kaka and Uncle waited with Aunty for pittuwala.

Mom was holding my hand firmly. We had to retrace the path where we had to slide over the trunk. The bodies had further decomposed overnight, attracting insects. We had to ignore the rotten stench and proceed further. As soon as we moved ahead, as expected, we came across a mountain that had caved in, God was testing us severely. Kaka, Uncle and Aunty, after waiting for a pittuwala for considerable time, decided to proceed. They were far behind us; we could not see them.

We came upon a slope, where we saw a waterfall because of which we had to spend a night at Jungle Chatti. While on our way up, there had been no waterfall. Heavy downpour had caused it, and it had taken a monstrous form, the force of which lowered the road by 5-7 ft. It was strewn with stones. Those brave-hearts who had risked the waterfall lay dead now. Many of the dead bodies were stuck partially, as we could either see their legs or heads. Water was making its way through the bodies, making them bloat like a big ball in the process; some of the limbs were seen dangling in the air. The scene was permanently etched in my mind as it would be the first and perhaps the last such in my life. With the kind help of other pilgrims, we could navigate through it. We stood ahead for Bini and Ba to negotiate the waterfall. We were happy that we had to cross just 2 km to Gaurikund and to freedom. However, Anant Drishti had envisaged a different plan altogether.

Kaka, Aunty and Uncle were also lucky to get a Pittu on the spot near the waterfall and helped Aunty to cross the waterfall. It was a big relief for Uncle and Kaka as otherwise Aunty would have found it difficult to cross the waterfall. The pittuwala helped her to cross the waterfall in a few seconds. Kaka's leg got sprained. He got hold of a stick from somewhere, which gave him great support in walking and crossing. We had been told by the shanty owners and doliwalas earlier that one should not stand at the same place and should keep moving ahead. We kept moving ahead without waiting for them.

We had hardly walked 100 metres when we saw another scene of mass destruction. We saw corpses lying in a haphazard manner. Many of them were in half decomposed state while some of them were totally decomposed. The bodies were strewn over 500-600 metres. The scene was deadly and ghostly. We felt as if we were passing through a battlefield, which eventually turned into an "S" shaped graveyard. The fear had gradually changed to dread and dismay now. But we kept our emotions under check and proceeded. I felt that Shankarji had taken up the incarnation of Kapalin who bears a string of skulls in the U shape (half S) around the neck. No wonder Shankarji is also known as Vinashak. We had to tread on the dead bodies for another 500 metres.

Mom was scared and she held my hand tightly. I consoled her saying if we want to stay alive we have to walk through it all. Bini, Lilaba and Jasmina, who were walking together, saw a man lying dead. White foam was oozing out from his mouth; they assumed that he might have died because of heart attack while crossing the jungle route. Next to him we saw a miniature red temple. Lord Shankar's Bhairav avatar was installed in the temple. The mountain above the temple is called Bhairav Chatti. This avatar of Lord Shiva is considered to be most dangerous and aggressive of all. He had actually manifested his Rudra Swarup by wiping out thousands of pilgrims.

At the start of the stretch we came across an obese boy who was from Bihar. His face was familiar to me because the other day, while standing the whole night in a shanty, we had seen him. He was standing there helplessly. He saw me and asked: *"Aap kahan se aaye, jungle ke raaste se aaye?"* (Did you come through the jungle?)

I: Nahi, ham jungle me bahaav rukne ke intezar me ruke the. Jaise hi bahaav kam hua ham wahan se chal ke aaye. (No, we waited for the flow to subside. The moment it stopped we came here walking). He was flabbergasted.

Bihari: *Ham woh 1 km paar karne ke liye puri raat jungle me thhe. Pure 24 ghante lage hame yahan pahunchne ko. Aur mera dost thha woh nahi mil raha; uske intezaar me khade hain. Hame kuchh pata nahi woh kaha atak gaya* (We were in the jungle all night just to cover 1 km. It took us 24 hours to reach here. We have lost our friend on the way. We are waiting for him not knowing where he is stuck.)

We realised that those who had ventured through Bhairav Chatti had slipped and fallen in the valley.

I turned back and looked at Bini twice. She was walking quietly without any expression. I knew if I uttered a single word now, she would break down. She was very scared. We saw people beating their chests lamenting the death of their near and dear ones; the sounds of which reverberated in the Garhwal region. At another turning, we saw an old man sitting on bent knees by a dead body. It was his wife. She was lying dead, face down. The man was much traumatised and weeping with his head bowed. Maybe he was cursing himself for having taken the decision of coming through the jungle route; otherwise she would have been alive. Most of the corpses were lying face down. Many of the dead bodies' eyes and mouths were still open. It was horrifying and terrifying. The whole area around the shrine had turned into a graveyard. Thanks to Bhairavnath.

We kept walking in the hope that we would just have to walk for an hour; thereafter we will be out of the mess. But that was not to be. Obviously God had some other plans for us. We had another waterfall on our way. It was like a never ending story now. We were getting used to overcoming one hurdle after another, our lives on tenterhooks. It became a regular game for us. Once you start the game it was mandatory to play the game. Crossing one hurdle after another made us realise that we had lived one full year as bonus every time. Each waterfall merited a different treatment. Slippery boulders had jammed the way. The only way to move forward was to climb over them. We had to sit on the slippery stones and slide forward. Then stand up on the two big stones and finally climb up the other side by stepping on slippery small stones. While doing this we had to support Mom and Lilaba too who were tired and fed up. They were finding it difficult to sit and stand up again and again. In desperation Lilaba asked Jasmina to leave her hand as she had already lived her life! Jasmina got angry with Lilaba. She got tensed.

I saw a local man coming our way. I asked him the distance to Gaurikund but he just stared at me and walked off. We stared walking ahead and came across another landslide where an uprooted tree had blocked the way along with the muddy and slippery stones. We had to go around the slope to cross. It was very slippery. Legs were knee-deep in the mud. It was an energy-sapping walk but we had to pass through it. We crossed nearly four serpentine slopes. We saw a huge crowd at a sharp slope, looking stunned and helpless. We proceeded towards the congregation to check the matter. We were stunned and amazed too. The patch of about 800 metres was in the process of obliteration due to a major landslide. It broke our hearts. We realised that there was no way out from the place. It was the end of the road for all of us. Nowhere to go! No way to go!. The chasm, gorge or abyss – whatever it was between Gaurikund and us - was too wide to cross. We were now concerned about Kaka, Uncle and Aunty as they were behind us and had not reached here yet. Anything could have happened in the meantime. We thought we may as well wait for another 15-20 minutes. If they do not reach here by then, we would start walking back in search of them.

As we were waiting for them we saw a man talking on a cell phone. It reminded us to check our cell phones, which were packed in plastic bags. We took them out and started pressing power button hard. One after another, we tried all of them. But to our dismay none of our cell phones were working. We approached him (Dayananad) and requested him to lend us his cell phone so that we could make a call. He refused outright. After many repeated pleadings and cajoling he lent us his cell phone. I could not offhand recollect anybody's number. After mentally practicing a few times I could recollect Bharti's number. I made a call to Bharti, my best friend. She picked up the call.

I: Hello Bharti, I am Ektaa. We are stranded on the way back to Gaurikund. Due to heavy rains, mountains have been swept away. We cannot proceed further as a mountain has toppled and plunged in the valley creating a huge void. There is no escape route. I am using someone else's phone. My phone is not working.

I blurted out in one breath.

Bharti: (She could not speak for a moment as was crying. She was overwhelmed by the magnitude of the problem). Do not move from there. I will call you back.

I: Relay the news to our relatives as I do not remember their numbers. (There was some noise) Also inform Natudada (grandpa). He will find a way. We are badly stuck. No way to move ahead.

Dayanand: *Usko bolo balance karwane ko. Phone me balance khatam ho gaya hain.* (Tell her to recharge the cell phone as the balance is low).

I: *Yep, Please top up the balance. Do it now.*

She hung up.

I realised that it was 6.30 am. After crossing the washed up mountains we felt as if half a day was over. It was a huge relief for both of us; we got to hear the voice of each other after four long days.

Next I called Padmanabhbhai and after repeating our details, informed him that Kaka, Uncle and Aunty had not joined us yet.

Padmanabh (delet in book) Padmanabhbhai: Do not loose courage. We are making all efforts to get you out. Take care of Kaka.

Immediately calls from relatives and friends started pouring in. A wave of relief spread amongst our relatives when they heard we were alive and safe. A pall of gloom lifted up and tears of joy welled up in their eyes.

I also had a word with Shilpaben, Lilaba's daughter (elder cousin). I could not stop myself from crying while talking to her. I went overboard when I spoke to her.

I: The mountains have slid into the valley all round. If the rains start again we may be no more. Just take us out of here somehow.

Shilpaben: Have faith in God and be calm.

Suddenly I heard Bini and Jasmina shouting and running back the way we had come. When I turned back, Kaka, Uncle and Aunty had reached. I was so happy to see them safe.. We were all overwhelmed to be together again. Jasmina and Bini hugged Kaka tightly.

Shilpaben: (Not knowing what was happening here; asked worriedly) What happened? Ektaa, Ektaa, please speak up.

I: (After a moment, happily) Kaka, Uncle and Aunty have joined us. We are all together now.

Shilpaben: Everything will be alright. Have courage. Together we shall fight the exigency and shall reach the pinnacle of success.

Hats off to Aunty for her courage and will power; she overcame all the hurdles and reached safely. We asked Uncle and Kaka to sit on a concrete bench, which was next to the landslide. Mom, Lilaba and Aunty rested on a dry gutter. I too followed them. However I was feeling very low as my leg was paining excruciatingly. I ignored the pain and concentrated on our finding ways to move out from here. Jasmina too had become very emotional and was losing her patience. She kept holding my hand tightly and managed to cry when no one was watching her.

Jasmina: What shall we do? How do we get out of here? Just think how Kaka, Mom and Lilaba must be suffering. I am feeling terribly sad. Despair is getting the upper hand over mind.

She turned her face lest Mom and Lilaba get worried seeing her.

I: Please cool down. We need to keep up our courage. If we think we can do it, we will do it. If we feel we will not be able to do then we shall never be able to do it.

We felt good after expressing our feelings to each other and gathered strength to fight back.

Everyone wanted to talk to their relatives. We were relieved to talk with our near and dear ones. Our relatives in turn were relieved. They cried with tears of joy. However they were given a big job of extricating us from the mess. The news spread like wild-fire about our wellbeing amongst our relatives and friends. Everyone started searching for friends in the government and corporate sectors who could apply pressure to the right people.

Padmanabhbhai called Shilpaben, who was so overwhelmed that she could not utter a word and started crying. She immediately took her car and left for Mumbai from Surat. Padmanabhbhai and Nikhil Jijjaji (Shilpaben's husband) booked their flight tickets from Mumbai to Dehradun. Nimeshbhai (my cousin) from Australia booked the tickets from Sydney-Delhi-Dehradun. Chintu Jijaji, Falguniben and Bhaveshbhai (USA) set the ball rolling for our rescue. Both Mama and masa from Ahmedabad booked tickets to Dehradun.

As we did not receive news for some time, feeling helpless at the moment, we started our own Operation Rescue by dialling the helpline numbers from Dayanand's cell phone. He was skinny and wheatish. He had a round face and wore spectacles. He is a tour operator. We started receiving calls from different family members; some of them from Mumbai, Ahmedabad and a few from the USA. Everyone was asking us the same question, "Give us your exact location," and "Can you come up to Gaurikund?" They all had no clue whatsoever about the location of the place where we were stuck; it was obviously not possible to walk further. Otherwise after walking for days, why would we seek help? We could have walked, if there had been any semblance of a road! Everyone was repeatedly asking us for our exact location, so we looked all around and found only destruction everywhere. To our surprise, Shivji had left us with one clue. Everything around was destroyed, but for one milestone. It said 'Gaurikund 1.5km' on one side and 'Kedarnath 12.5 km'. We immediately informed Shilpaben.

I: Shilpaben we are exactly 1.5 km from Gaurikund

Shilpaben: Ok. We shall rescue you from there.

She hung up. She did not pay attention to what we were saying! (She felt we were stuck somewhere in the middle of nowhere, so could not be so precise!)

She called again.

Shilpaben: Do you see anything around?

I: Why do you ask?

Shilpaben: If we come to know where you are located we can inform the military personnel to dispatch the choppers.

I: We are exactly 1.5 km from Gaurikund.

Shilpaben: How do you know the exact kilometre?

I: Shilpaben there is a milestone indicating Gaurikund 1.5 km.

Shilpaben: Are you sure there is a milestone?

I: Yep, 100 per cent

Shilpaben: Okay.

Everybody was overwhelmed and helpless. We felt like beggars who had lined up for food to be served. Richa, a girl from Odisha, was with her mother and grandmother. They had come as a group of nine, but did not know the fate of the other six members. She was distributing chocolates to everyone. When she reached Kaka, he could not help the tears welling up. He felt till now he had been distributing biscuits, water and chocolates. Today this small girl was serving him. He was reluctant to accept it. His eyes turned red, he could not stop crying.

When we told Kaka how everyone back home was making all efforts to rescue us from our predicament, his eyes flooded with tears. He cried out openly. He felt blessed the way family members had come together to rescue us. Family happiness is the real happiness. He had a sprained muscle resulting in a painful walk.

Stranded pilgrims were a helpless lot. They wanted to speak to their family members. A few of them had already lost their family members and a few of them were not aware about the plight of their family; whether they were alive or not. We had only Dayanand's cell phone; its battery level was getting low. We were worried that once the cell phone stops working we would be disconnected from our family members who were working for our rescue. The cell phone was the only medium to remain connected. While we were making efforts an old man from Jharkhand approached us. He was very negative in his thoughts. He asked us to stop making futile calls to the Government employees as they would not be doing anything for us. We ignored him initially and concentrated on our work. He would not relent. Finally Jasmina and I sarcastically said, "*Agar aapne abhi ek shabda bhi bola to ham aapko yahan se niche fenk denge, sidhe nadi me chale jaaoge.*" (If you utter a single word we shall throw in the river.) He just laughed and walked off.

A man with his two young daughters came to us. One of his daughters enquired curiously, "*Didi hum yahan se nikal paayenge ya nahi?*" (Will we be rescued?) I looked into her eyes and replied gently, wiping away her tears, "*Daro mat, hum yahan se zaroor niklenge, isiliye hum logo ko phone laga rahe hai.*" (Do not worry; we shall definitely be rescued. That's why we calling people.)

We were struggling to be rescued from here. To get noticed by the chopper, we lit a fire to enable the pilot to locate our position. We also fashioned a flag out of a red coloured cloth to wave it in the air when a chopper passes by to draw their attention. We were struggling. However the lady who gave us the red cloth was time and again drying her clothes over it. We tried to convince her not to do so. Every two minutes she came and kept another cloth on the red cloth for drying. It was actually a test of patience for all of us. Her purpose seemed to dry her clothes, and nothing more. It seemed she did not understand our language. She smiled each time we got annoyed! She was so innocent that she was not at all worried about getting out. We found many such strange characters.

Amongst the pilgrims there was a lady who was crying uncontrollably. She approached us seeking our help. She recounted that she wanted to carry her sister's body home. She had even hired a pittuwala to ferry her but he had left them in a lurch. She was crying because she was forced to leave her sister's body behind. If she cannot take home the body she may take her own life. Lilaba could not see her grief; she tried to pacify her. She explained her that this is Devbhoomi; anyone who lost his or her soul would directly go to Heaven. Listening to Lilaba's explanation she got agitated; accusing us to be heartless and saying that because we had not lost any family member, we cannot understand her pain. She walked away crying. Maybe she was right. We should have shown more empathy than sympathy.

One after another we came across many such grieving persons. People were disoriented; losing their patience. The hunger of three to four days made them angrier. Till 4 o'clock in the evening we called up many people back home as well as many Government officials for help. We kept receiving calls as well. We also called up many news channel reporters, whose numbers were furnished from Mumbai (home). However, all our efforts were going in vain. The battery was too low by now and the phone could switch off any time. We started pleading for batteries and cell phones from the few people around us; but everyone was reluctant. At the end we got lucky and some of them agreed to lend their cell phones the next day.

It was dusk and we realised and made up our mind that we had to stay here another night. With no food or water, no blankets or shelter it was going to be a challenge staying in the open at night. Yesterday we had some space to take shelter; today there was nothing available. Consider it: under the open skies, amidst glacial and frigid Himalayan cold, with only damp clothes, exposed to gusty gales; all salient features to remain awake.

An "S" shaped patch had formed on either side of the mountains slope that had been swept away; around 1,000 people had gathered in the 1.5 km stretch by late evening. At the end of the curve, public toilets were situated. Due to the landslide the toilets had broken down completely, including the side door which also got broken. The situation was grim and dour as well as dismal and gloomy. We had to overcome this challenge. No situation can be classified as good or bad. It is the attitude that makes it so.

We also came across a Hyderabadi Aunty whose bag containing Rs 25,000 cash was snatched by Nepali guys. She got separated from her group member. She was alone. We met yet another girl whose leg got fractured in a landslide in the Jungle Chatti area. There was another group of eight led by one Prabhuji. We were a group of unknown people living together due to the cruel conspiracy of the circumstances, destined to know each other and live together. We were hapless, fatigued, jaded, exhausted and a weary lot badly shaken, stirred, stranded and helpless, aiming for a single target; to be out of here as soon as possible. However, we were a hopeful and an upbeat lot who had all the hopes to be rescued very shortly. Nowhere to go and nowhere to sleep.

We began gathering wood. There was a shanty owner who had left the shanty in a hurry to save his life. People dismantled the wooden frames and uncovered the plastic for their own usage during the night. In no time all traces of the existence of shanty had vanished. People helped to carry the planks but some had the gumption to steal our wooden planks. When we objected they did not bother.

Presently I tried to rest my sore feet. The shoes needed much coaxing before it came off. My feet were very swollen as if I had contracted elephantiasis. Everyone got worried. Was it an insect bite; was it poisonous? It may spread through the body. While crossing landslides when the leg got stuck in the mud and while taking the leg out of the mud, my calves got lacerated by the branches. However there was no ointment to apply!

We rustled up a bonfire to warm us up in unbearable cold. We were just praying that there would be no rains tonight. Lo and behold the rains showed up again with impunity. We tried to protect the flames from extinguishing by adding the ghee I had with me. We chanted Gayatri Mantra, Mrityunjay mantras and shlokas the whole night.

Life Struggle, Day-1

June 19, 2013 Day 15

At the first ray of sun, everyone got up. Bini greeted me with a nervous gesture and the first thing she asked was, "Will we be able to get out today from here? I don't think so." I asked her to be calm and have faith in God. The day started with hope and faith; in any case, we would be rescued today. We were waiting for the clock to strike 9, time to call the military people, help lines and our family members. Our family members had already started Operation Rescue from 6 am. Bharati tried to find out contacts of news agencies, and Maharashtra Disaster Management Authority. Other family members were trying to contact different government and military camps but to no avail. They then brought in Prince and Nishant from Mumbai (family friends).

As described by Falguniben after watching the news, Prince and Nishant realised the gravity of the problem. She sent Prince and Nishant to Delhi where they tried to contact the relevant political leaders, but as they made no headway, they rushed to Dehradun. Padmanabhbhai broke down on hearing this as their efforts did not bear any fruit. With great difficulty everybody consoled him. Even in Dehradun there was no discernible progress as they could not achieve much.

We were waiting since 4 am. Everybody had a single agenda; how to clear out of here fast. As I was down with high fever I was sleeping on Mom's lap who held me tightly because I was shivering very much. I was feeling so low that I could not contribute much towards the Operation Rescue. Jasmina was doing the running about. She connected us with our relatives. People came to us enquiring about the current situation. A few of them used to talk nicely and others just stared at us.

Our big problem was to get hold of a mobile with full battery. We contacted old men who point blank refused to lend their phones. Later we managed to convince an old man to lend his mobile for today's use. Initially he was not ready. We told him calmly that if he refused to lend his mobile, we will not be able to rescue him. He got apprehensive and gave his mobile for the common cause.

Surprisingly, we saw a few Nepalis walking through a path which no one dared to tread before. We crowded around them to elicit information, which was not very encouraging. Dayanand tricked one of them to sell his mobile. We clicked a few photographs of the dead pilgrims and the surroundings with the new mobile.

Our family members, who were more concerned than us, were making all out efforts to get food and medicine packets dropped. They were calling us frequently to know whether we were receiving the food items. We informed them that we have not received anything as yet. Dayanand felt that our family members were simply making calls and not doing anything effective or fruitful. He discontinued lending us his cell phone. He chose to stay away from us. Perhaps we would have also reacted in the same manner. As it is said; if God closes a door on you, he simultaneously opens another for you.

Jasmina and Dayanand decided to check the upper reaches to gauge the number of people who had gathered. Luckily while coming back, Jasmina met one Taneja Uncle talking on a cell phone. As he was not well versed in English, he requested Jasmina to talk to the caller. He gave us his cell phone for our use without much ado. It opened a door for us. We were not known to many people but everybody came to know us as we were leading the Operation Rescue. He would sit on a slope above us on the hill. Whenever the phone rang he would come down and inform us that Didi (Shilpaben) had called.

Taneja Uncle had memorised Shilpaben's number so he would pick up her calls selectively. Initially he used to get annoyed by the too frequent calls but he realised that the calls were regarding reaching essential supplies to us. Presently we received a call from Shilpaben informing that they have arranged for a private chopper for our rescue, which was parked at Dehradun. She informed me that they were yet to get the permission from the authorities. We were feeling very happy that today we will be out from here. I relayed the good news to the other members of my family, cautioning them against revealing it to anyone else as yet.

After waiting for more than two hours we called up Shilpaben to know the latest. She said they were working on the matter. She asked us to keep our strength and will-power intact. She informed us that they have offered the authorities the usage of the chopper free of cost for a few days, once our family gets rescued safely. I abruptly asked her how they would rescue us as there was no space for landing the chopper. She said they will airlift us. I said okay.

Elsewhere Nishant and Prince were left fretting and wringing their hands in Dehradun. They realised that just phoning was not going to help us. No one will ever present anything readymade on the platter till you work for it. They decided to call Chintu Jiju in USA to arrange for a chopper in Dehradun. The idea was to reach as near as possible to us; thereon walk up the remaining distance.

This enthused Prince. Young blood surged as he contacted Jijaji. He conveyed all the information given by Nishant. Jijaji was non-committal and hung up.

Jasmina and I conveyed the information to the rest of the family members. Uncle's think-tank had started ticking as fast as the Rajdhani train. He started posing various questions to Kaka. When they dropped the ladder for air-lifting it would sway in windy conditions caused by the rotating chopper blades. It would be impossible for him to climb the ladder. Further it would be difficult for Malti as well as both his bhabhis. We all started laughing. He even told Kaka, "Rajnibhai, as I am wearing loose pants, when I hold the ladder to climb in such heavy winds, my pants will come off!!" There was lots of laughter which freshened up the droopy and gloomy faces. We laughed hard, till tears came to our eyes. It was two hours of non-stop laughter in the royal court (Darbar) of Laughter. You score brownie points if you can bring laughter in a gloomy situation. Uncle helped us by lightening the atmosphere.

Like the Stone Age we became aware of the mornings, noon, afternoons and evenings by the position of sun during the day. After a long wait in the afternoon, we saw the first helicopter of Pawan Hans coming towards us. We all ran close to it thinking it was for our rescue. We were overjoyed. We wanted to go ahead and scream Patel, Patel, to enable them to know our position. As the chopper lowered, it chopped off the tree branches due to the air pressure, resulting in the insects and dust getting sprayed on us. We wished to look up and communicate with them but we were not able to open our eyes due to the whirlpool of dust. Clothes hung for drying flew away. We did not see much as we could not blink often. People were very much excited seeing the chopper. This was the first signal that we have a chance of getting out of this place. It was a slim ray of hope after the last two dark days.

Suddenly a box filled with eatables fell down. Everyone rushed to grab it. Everyone wanted to have a go at it. It was a free for all. Half the packets were going down the valley. "*Sab niche ja raha hain; kya kar rahe ho?*" (What are they doing;

everything is going down the valley). We tried to get closer and catch the packets. However, as the road was wrecked and the trees occupied rest of the areas, we were not receiving the packets. Most of them went straight down the valley.

Screams emanated from empty bellies. People who were starving for the last three days could not stand the sight of food going to dumps. Everyone got chastened and humbled.

One gunny bag had fallen on the back of an old man who was sitting down. He fell forward on his face. No one bothered to help the old man. Instead they were jumping over him to catch the packets. People were literally fighting and snatching the packets from each other's hands. Uncle also ventured to join in but backed out as he could not muster enough courage to join in the fray. Jasmina, Dayanand and I ran, but what can girls do in the men's crowd? There is a proverb *'daane daane pe likkha hain khaanewale ka naam'* – every grain has the name of the person written on it, which is destined for him. Every incident happens as per the wishes of God. Food packet will go to the destined person. A packet luckily landed at Jasmina's feet and Dayanand also managed to get one. The chopper crew was indiscriminately ejecting the packets and was not monitoring where the packets were landing. People were cursing the crew; thankfully they could not hear over the excruciatingly high noise. It was a difficult task for them too as the area was surrounded by trees and just 8-10 ft wide road to drop the parcels in. They were working for a good cause but their best efforts were going in vain. The effect of devastation had made the victims behave like animals, the only difference was that they were just fighting and not killing each other. We could get two packets consisting of three puris in each packet between 20 people. It was as tough as getting pearls from the ocean.

We shared the 'booty' amongst 20 people. We shared a few pieces of puris amongst ourselves.

It was a testing time for everyone. Our family in the US had organised *Triambakji Path* by the local Maharajshri to help us face hardships with minimum effort. Chintu Jijaji, after consulting, gave Prince and Nishant the go-ahead to make arrangement for a chopper. Prince and Nishant also readied their trekking equipment.

The entire atmosphere for the whole day was a mixed bag of emotions. After sustaining two nights with practically no food and water, there was a slim ray of hope on the horizon. Seeing the chopper moving around and going back without rescuing us made people more aggressive and frustrated. With each passing moment they were becoming impatient. People were coming up with different types of ideas and plans but we knew that the only plan which can work was God's plan. Some of them got the news that choppers were plying frequently between Kedarnath and Gaurikund. Some suggested that we walk back to Kedarnath for an early rescue. But obviously it was not a viable idea. By now the roads leading to Kedarnath would have been wiped out completely.

After sometime we received a call from Shilpaben. She asked me, "Can you walk back to Kedarnath?" I paused for a second and firmly said, "Not possible." For a moment all hurdles that we had faced streamed alive in our eyes; all those waterfalls, landslides - the rivulets. I knew how we had managed to come through. We had become puppets strung on a thin thread whose control was in the hands of God. We had struggled with ourselves, our fears and our physical constraints before reaching here. There was no possibility of walking back 12.5 kms.

Dayanand's cell phone battery got over. I felt depressed. The mobile was the only hope of our survival. It was a medium of connection between us and the outer world. I was feeling totally blank and nervous. I could not help crying. I said, "Shilpaben, this is our last call; if you are doing anything for us then you must do it before sunset or just leave us to our fate. We shall come back if it is so fated." We knew that our family was doing their best and like us they also would be despondent by evening. We were very clear that after 4 o'clock, rescue operation would be halted. We were preparing for another night here.

People were famished and weak, and looked gaunt and haggard. They found chana meant for the horses, wetted it in the river water and try to satiate their hunger. Uncle also had some, which reminded us of the time when he had refused them saying they were meant for the horses and today he was requesting people for chana. At times we may lose everything overnight but we must not lose our courage and keep on trying. One has to adjust according the circumstances. Pride leads to downfall. It reminded me of a Hindi song *diwana aadmi ko banaati hai rotia (The (search of) bread (food) makes man crazy).*

The difficulties were increasing. The scene around us was becoming more nerve-racking as people had started dying. Weak, infected, injured and famished, old people were the first victims. I saw an old man's corpse lying near the broken toilet. He must have vomited blood as his face was smeared with dried blood. Many of them had become unidentifiable. Dead bodies were stinking horribly. We also got news of four people dying on the upper slope. A group of people came with a dead body chanting *"raam bolo bhai raam"* and threw it in the valley. It sent shivers down our bodies. Dayanand asked them to check the belongings before throwing, so that the family members can be informed. They bluntly refused, fearing infection as they did not know how many days ago they had died. Bodies had started stinking, and if they did not throw them, others will fall sick. They 'advised' us to inspect the body ourselves if we were so interested. We requested them to throw a dead body which was lying on our slope. They refused to do so as it was not their work. It was on our slope; we had to throw it. Under adverse circumstances, division of land and their possession was already taking place.

Meanwhile Jasmina had a word with Bharti in Mumbai. Jasmina asked her surprised, "Are you not going to office? Every time I call you, you answer immediately!" Bharti apparently was coordinating things from home. She felt bad and told her, "You people are my family and you are more important than work." Jasmina realised truly that a "friend in need is a friend in deed."

Presently Dayanand got up and said, "There is no chance of getting out today; God knows when we will be able to get out from here. We have to go in search of essentials." Dayanand and Prabhuji went uphill in search of food, water and anything that would extend our life on the hill.

They returned after two to three hours. They brought three big plastic sheets, biscuit packets and two to three milk bottles. When they arrived, others approached them and begged for biscuits. Prabhuji and an old man from his group were managing the crowd, and got mobbed.

In the meantime I was shocked to see the same old man selling the biscuits bought by Dayanand and Prabhuji who had walked up a strenuous 3 km stretch. We were very irritated. I could not stop myself and forbade him from doing it. Instead he shouted me down. When I threatened him that I had seen him selling, he shouted louder. I asked his daughter to look into the matter since what he was doing was unethical. She informed me that he had a mental problem. She asked us to leave the matter to her. One must realise and accept one's mistakes, which will help improve one self. The mistakes committed by others make us angry. And also our mistakes make us feel guilty.

It was late evening but it felt like night. Not a single light could be seen for miles around. Insects had taken over the night shift from the chirping birds. They were also 'homeless' like us. They were busily buzzing making weird and bizarre sounds. All the owners had left their horses behind and ran off to save their lives. It is true that humans are selfish. The horses were their bread earners and it was surprising to see the horses abandoned in such deplorable conditions. Like us, the horses too were searching for food. But who would provide them? They were with us. While sleeping on a very narrow road there was hardly any space left for horses to move around. We had to make some space for their movement. Due to narrow lane, whole night we were worried if the horses would step on us. Due to their twinkling eyes we could see their movements.

We used the plastic sheets brought by Dayanand and Prabhuji as shelter. Two of them were put down on the floor. The third one was used as a roof. Two sides were tied to a railing and the other two sides were tied with the help of a bamboo with the support of stones. Thus a structure was created. It was insufficient to accommodate 20 people, but would give us shelter if it were to rain again. As the night closed on us; the temperature dipped alarmingly. To mitigate our cold, we lit up a small bon-fire which is an art. Dayanand's wife seemed to be an expert as she lit the wood in a minute. We settled down enjoying the warmth emanating from the bonfire.

During the day we received many calls from Mumbai and US and other military officials who were organising the Operation Rescue. Each phone call created a sense of relief initially, but after 4 pm, everything seemed worthless. In the morning we were sure we would be out of here, but can we challenge God's plans which dictates our every step? It was our fate that in spite of booking the tickets twice earlier, we could not make it. We wanted to go to Nainital but Shivji had other plans for us as he drew us here. It increased my faith in Shivji.

Once you wish to do something, the universe aligns to help you achieve your goal. You connect with good Samaritans like selfless Dayanand who lighten your worries and anxieties. He was benevolent and obliging to even people who were not his own. Such people are scarce. We shall always be indebted to our angel who was aptly named Dayanand. It is better to spread the fragrance of your personality rather than some artificial perfume.

All day long Prince and Nishant shopped and gathered all necessary things useful for trekking to the nearest point. Chintu Jijaji's efforts ultimately fructified into wangling permission for operating the chopper. Since it was already evening, they made arrangements for the chopper to take off by early morning.

Shilpaben informed us, "Military officers have started climbing up your route and by tomorrow morning they would reach you. Do not lose hope. We have hired private trekkers as well; they will also reach soon. We are trying our best." She exhorted us to accept our miserable conditions and inculcate confidence in all. "Your intrinsic energy will help you to overcome the external ordeals," she said encouragingly.

I got a place closest to the railings. Here the undulating draught-like gale created by the flowing of Mandakini's ice cold water between the mountains was wafting up. Everybody was sleeping in a foetal position to conserve the warmth.

The person who fought with me was now claiming my space as his own. My leg was bad and I could not get up. Prabhuji told him to sleep elsewhere. He tried to sleep between Jasmina and Bini but had to give up as there was no space.

Every sunset questioned the accounts of opportunities lost even as sunrise brought in fresh ones. With only one thing in mind – to get out from here – we all tried to sleep with open eyes!!!

Life Struggle, Day-2

JUNE 20, 2013 DAY 16

Everybody woke up with the first rays of sun. It was 4.30 in the morning. Our watches also were ticking as per God's watch in His place. It was a bright sunny day after three days of continuous downpour. The day started with positive vibes and hope as I had immense faith in Shilpaben's promise. Military will definitely arrive.

Bini hugged me from behind and asked me the same question she had asked the previous day; what would be the fate of our rescue? I smiled and nodded positively. I had high hopes as Shilpaben had assured me that the military were on their way. The mind reasoned that it was not possible to construct the road or build a new makeshift helipad in a day. Still, hope soared high. We could not see any movement from military personnel. The mobile phone battery was dead.

PG Uncle, who could not control his hunger, went up the slope on the hillside in search of tea. He managed to find a cup of tea. He offered tea to Kaka saying, "It is a half cup tea, so we will get one sip each." Nepali guys came every day; Hyderabadi Aunty would start abusing them. Listening to her for three continuous days, we teased her by mimicking.

Elsewhere at 7 am, after completing the formalities, the chopper landed in Sirsi from Dehradun as a military chopper had met with an accident in Rudraprayag. Prince and Nishant drove to Rudraprayag in a jeep. They could not display the same courage in the mountainous region as they had shown in Sirsi. Their bravado of rescuing us by climbing the mountain bottomed out in Rudraprayag.

Like the chilling cold, the scorching sun was in its full glory; people now had started removing their woollens. Kaka removed his three rain suits for drying in the sun. We all had become inhabitants of the place! People had acclimatised to the conditions well. People made good use of sunlight by drying their clothes on the railing. The heat was gradually increasing. In fact, it was burning our skin. The intensity was so high that later on we had to take shelter under the tree. We started our search for safe drinking water as nobody had brushed their teeth for three days.

It was the third day at the same place and there were no signs of any help from military or the evacuation teams. Uncle from Jharkhand went up the slope and found a PVC water pipe with water flowing from it. We thought it was fresh water coming from the tank kept above. When we were about to fill the water bottle, Dayanand cautioned us as it was not potable. Better not to drink it as we were unaware of the source of the water.

People had started polluting the place by defecating and spitting. They were so adamant they would not listen to reason. We were exasperated. We screamed at them every time, but to no avail. Furthermore, some village women came by and started washing their clothes in the dropping water. We felt annoyed but we were helpless. We were desperately waiting for military to arrive.

In meantime, Bini saw the old man who had fought with me stuffing packets of biscuits and milk bottles in his bag bought by Dayanand the other day. Bini showed me what he was doing. Bini was angry and ordered him to stop doing it as she cannot bear any hanky-panky. Maybe he was out of earshot; he did not pay any attention to her. Bini got frustrated and pleaded with him to refrain from pilfering. The man in turn got angry and showered his anger on her by shouting aloud. I asked Bini to avoid him and ignore the matter as he was old.

Prince and Nishant reached Rudraprayag. They were astounded by the death and destruction around them. Barren grounds, broken roads, dilapidated houses and river-swept villages were enough to bring out the strongest emotions of dismay and panic in their impressionable minds. Knees knocking and heart ready to back out, they steeled their mind to march forward and complete the job for which they had come this far. After walking 2 km on the cracked roads from Rudraprayag they reached a bank of river which was flowing at a high speed. Here at the confluence, Triveni Sangam, the three rivers were competing with each other for speed. A special squad of military had arrived and immediately started Operation Rescue. Looking around they realised the importance of self-preservation. They were trying to come to terms with the situation. They stood there wondering whether they were witnessing a nightmare with open eyes!

On one hand, in Rudrapryag, Prince and Nishant were working overtime. On the other side Padmanabhbhai, Jijaji and mama were busy organising the dropping of boxes with medicine and food items. Shilpaben was coordinating the arrangements on the phone. Bharati was gathering information from news channels and disaster management. Friends and relatives were exercising their best efforts and time. They all were praying to god for our rescue.

It was afternoon time. The moment the chopper was spotted, people rushed madly towards it to grab the boxes. They were fighting amongst themselves causing a mini stampede. Due to the prolonged hunger they had lost all sense of humanity. They just wanted to assuage the fire in their families' belly. They did not mind picking the packets which had fallen on the dead bodies or on the faeces. Some of them were torn. It was a battle of survival with no end date. Though they were hungry for four days, strangely no one contracted acidity or giddiness! If this is not a miracle then what it is? Suffice to say this was God's land! Jasmina and I got up; she exhorted me to take care of my leg and made me sit. Just then a packet landed in her hand. Uncle was overjoyed and immediately kept it near our group. Bini analysed the situation well; she opened up the packets and hid the contents near each one's leg.

Two Bihari boys shared their experience of walking and surviving through the jungle area with me. Their hands were swollen like a potato due to a splinter ridden palm. While snatching the food packets, the content fell down and was trodden over by the people running around. One of them collected two pieces of puris. It was unclean, since it was covered with soil. He was removing the soil while talking to me. "Take it. Eat it." His friend was not sure whether it was edible. But the first one persuaded, "You have not eaten for four days, so eat whatever you are getting or else we may die of hunger." Clouds of sympathy started fanning out. It was very heart touching. People give importance to things which are difficult to achieve. Situation forces people to live accordingly.

Down below the military personnel were building a small wooden bridge over the river. They placed two huge trunks across the river creating two paths for crossing. The river was raging and boisterous; even a Volvo Bus would have been swept away in its wake!

Meanwhile, a group of six to seven men marched angrily towards us claiming that we have got many packets of food stashed away. They asked us to give it to them. We countered that we did not have any. They would not listen and started throwing our belongings around. We explained that we are 20 of us and for the last three days we had not had anything; no need to fight with us. Since they were not convinced they inspected the area around us. As they did not find anything, they returned empty handed.

Bini called me, "Ektaa, come here, have something." The small packet had two pieces of puri, sweet boondi, one torn Frooti and a few biscuits. I asked her to share the two puris with the Bihari boys as they were starving. I gave it to them. We were left with a packet of biscuit. A little girl came up and requested us to give her something to eat. She said her younger brother was hungry and it would be good if we can help her. Bini and I went with her and gave two biscuits to her brother. We were left with one puri which we shared with a strange feeling of satisfaction and peace of mind. Seeing the Biharis snacking after four days and trying to fill in their empty bellies touched my heart. There is nothing like helping others in one's moment of grief. I felt good by offering them freedom from hunger, albeit temporarily.

Uncle was delighted to see sweet boondi. He was sleeping or lying awake most of the time, but suddenly woke up sensing the aroma of boondi around. He had boondi along with puri; he did not feel shy to ask Dayanand for pickle. It was a grand celebration akin to 56 bhog for Uncle in the Kedarnath valley. He could not have been happier.

Shortly Prince and Nishant mustered enough courage to surge ahead. Their grit and guts were commendable. They were well equipped with SIM cards of almost all service providers. Unfortunately, none of the cell phones were working due to the mayhem. They could not contact their families for days on end.

After having some food we started a clean-up operation of the entire area. Uncle too pitched in with the help of a stick. He would collect all the garbage with the stick and then throw it down the hillside. Bini saw Kaka shivering in a corner. She told me to attend to Kaka. His eyes were red; filled with tears. He was very weak and seemed helpless and guilty that he could not help his daughters in any manner. Generally, Kaka is a very active person. Watching him immobilised due to his painful leg without uttering a single word left me in deep shock and regret. I was feeling sorry for him. Bini could not see his condition and broke down. Finally I also broke down. As he could not trim, his moustache and beard had grown haphazardly. His clothes were soiled due to long wear and tear. No daughter would remain unmoved seeing the pitiable state of her father. I was deeply touched and perturbed by the hardship he faced after giving us all the affordable luxuries in our life and bringing up like princesses.

Thick friends Prince and Nishant started walking along the coconut tree wooden trunk placed across the river. Prince saw Nishant coming after him. Their eyes met. If they could not negotiate the river, was it a bye bye for now ? Both were diffident and timid; they got goose-pimples. They were perspiring in the chilly conditions. They were offering words of courage to each other. Prince spread his hands for balance and took tentative steps; he did not dare look back now. Suddenly a screw from the trekking stick fell from Nishant's hand and struck the wooden plank. He lost his balance looking at the falling screw. He was shivering all over as he saw his end flickering before his eyes. Prince called out his name. It was a very delicate moment. However Nishant ran the remaining four steps and landed safely on the ground. In a moment they gathered themselves and hugged each other.

They took a few steps looking at the mountains on the opposite side. Pilgrims looked like ants moving. Prince remarked that this seemed easy so let us climb it in a jiffy. Young blood had no fear of consequences. Prince started walking in a reverie while Nishant stood rooted looking up the mountain. Abruptly the same mountain gave way without any warning over the pilgrims like a pack of cards and flattened them like ants. While walking they were caught unawares under the shower of debris of stones and boulders. They were mashed to pulp.

Nishant pulled Prince back. When Prince turned around he saw the mayhem, both were stunned and stupefied. All their enthusiasm and bravado waned and faded into thin air after witnessing the ghastly incident. Morale dropped like dry leaves in autumn. They had witnessed death at first hand and were thoroughly shaken and stirred. They had no fear of death but now they were not sure. They could gauge the extent of damage and destruction. They realised the Destructive Power of Shivji, who is also known as Vinashak. They truly understood the magnitude of the problem only now, and this made them more worried about our safety and security. However they decided to work with renewed vigour.

Nishant: Should we go ahead?

Prince*:* Yep, let's do it.

Nishant*:* It will be in their interest if we can make arrangements here for saving them. If we are alive we shall help them out.

Hearing this, Prince sobered down.

Jasmina was talking with Shilpaben; PG Uncle frenziedly snatched the phone from her hand and started requesting, "Shilpaben, expedite whatever you want to do as our health is deteriorating. Rajnibhai is also not well." This created panic amongst our family members.

The entire day and night aunty would lie down with closed eyes. We asked her several times to have something, but she would not have anything at all. She is diabetic and on insulin. For the past four days she didn't have any medicine or insulin. We were worried for her health. Lilaba was treasurer of food who would conserve the food for emergency. There were different characters in our group who would vie for importance. One was Bini who was dejection personified. Then there was Richa from

Odisha who was bubbly and effervescent and talking of having *chaat* and manicure and pedicure once she was rescued.

We had a senior Rajasthani couple carrying necessary utensils. They would cook rice daily. Today we saw them applying Ponds cream to avoid cracking of skin! We were at a loss as to how to react. One must happily overcome any difficulty that comes your way. Difficulties may always be there around you like the air, but your intrinsic energy can blow it away and triumph over it.

Everyone had diverse views and concepts about life, and living through emergency is the specialty of man. One can spend the entire life crying while others can make light of the problem and live a positive life. People who always complain can never expect to be happy.

We realised that we were not going to be rescued soon. Dayanand asked Jasmina and Bini to go along with him in search of food, I was not able to walk properly so I stayed back. They crossed the damaged narrow road ahead of us surpassing the big stones and faeces. The walking path was narrow, with space only to keep one foot at a time. Bini backed out after seeing the cracked road.

An one old Uncle came to enquire about rescue operation. When he saw my swollen leg he went back and came with an ointment. He advised me to apply it so that the swelling would subside. Another Uncle came along and enquired, "What should I do?" He also had a daughter like me but had lost her while coming the jungle way. "I gave her my hand as she slipped, but her hand slipped out of mine and she fell on the stone smashing her head." We cried inconsolably and wondered how he would manage as her image appears in front of him day in and day out. He was in quandary whether to live or end his life. The least I could do was to offer consolation. God, please do not let even our enemies suffer in such a manner. The father would be carrying the burden of loss all his life.

Nikhil Jijaji called Prince.

Nikhil Jijaji: Where are you? We are trying to call you for the last five hours. You have not tried even once.

Prince speaking slowly: As there was no network I could not call. We are okay. (Prince did not feel right recounting the mayhem as it would spread panic.)

Nikhil Jijaji: We think you should come back immediately. Do not proceed further. Wherever you are, come back.

Prince heaved a sigh of relief.

Today Kaka could stand up to wash his face. I told Kaka we need to throw the body which was lying nearby or it will start stinking. Kaka and Uncle, with the help of the two Bihari boys, threw the dead body down in the Mandakini River, chanting prayers.

After an hour Jasmina and Dayanand came back holding two wet blankets in their hands. The blankets seemed to have been immersed in muck and smelt. When we asked them where from they brought it they just smiled. They did not reveal that it was lifted from the dead bodies. Uncle took one of them. Another we gave to Aunty. We had given two blankets to sadhus so we too received two blankets. What goes out invariably comes back. As you sow, so shall you reap. Even after he experiences the profound truth, if he still has no faith in God then what can we say about such a man? Kaka had also offered biscuits so he also received a packet without any effort or argument or fight. When God protects man, he remains protected. I bow a thousand times to God.

It was evening now. Taneja Uncle continued to receive calls from my family. Meanwhile a south Indian lady from upper slope came running and crying in front of Kaka. She was weeping and speaking something incoherently in her language. Everyone was shocked to see her coming to Kaka when there were so many people around. There are no easy answers for some questions.

We were looking at her intently. Through Hyderabadi Aunty we came to know that her father-in-law had just passed away. Her father-in-law and she had got separated from their group. She was asking Kaka to help her in throwing the dead body into the river. We asked her to calm down and not to cry as we would surely help her. We offered her financial help but she refused. With the help of the two Bihari boys, the body was disposed off. Later on Hyderabadi aunty told Lilaba about how she was looted by the Nepali guys on her way. She was not left with single penny. All the same Lilaba offered her Rs 500. Lilaba told me about it and I informed Kaka. He too gave her another Rs 2,000 so that she can reach home comfortably.

Prince and Nishant were struggling to return. Suddenly a house on the mountain got swept away as if made up of paper. People and the special jawans were dumbfounded. People panicked and ran helter-skelter. One couple was walking down with their child. The child who was walking a few steps ahead saw her parents getting smashed by a huge boulder. The child stood stupefied watching the boulder for a minute and then started crying uncontrollably. A jawan ran and picked her up consoling her, patting her back. Many others also died in the mishap. The jawan ran amuck and was on rampage. A woman was impatient to cross the bridge forcibly. The jawan slapped her. Walking waywardly the jawan sat near the stone where Prince and Nishant were standing.

The previous night Dayanand and his wife could not sleep the whole night. He requested us to remove the third plastic and keep it on the ground so that everyone can sleep and relax. Again the same old man started yelling, not allowing us to remove the plastic. This time around Dayanand had enough and shouted him down. He made the old man realise that it was he who had brought the plastic and not the other way round. The old man would not listen and challenged Dayanand. Finally, the old man's daughter and Prabhuji intervened and calmed him.

With lots of things happening on the same day, everyone was tired; still there was no sign of military without which no rescue was possible from here. Everyone had one point agenda - to get out as soon as possible. During meditation there arrives a time when you do not hear or see anything; achieving a steady state of equilibrium. Shivji is the Master of Meditation. We could feel the presence. We were never troubled by negative thoughts. In spite of going through the grind, we had experienced a strange peace of mind.

We again lit a bonfire and tried to warm the cold and fatigued bones.

Dayanand enquired how we managed to come by the jungle route; we told him that we had come by crossing the waterfall. He remarked that he had never seen such a treacherous path and never would. It took 24 hours walking the ghostly deserted road in the dark. He could not bear to talk about it and his hair stood on its ends.

The rain drops falling on the stones and the dry leaves were making weird sounds. People treading on leaves and shifting of stones added to the eeriness. Families crying out for their dear and near ones in trouble echoed, making the atmosphere haunting. Bodies hanging from the trees were dripping blood, or was it dew drops? It was difficult to judge. People were trying to rest, leaning on the trunk of a tree for support. For all we knew, there could be a few bodies hanging from the same tree!!! Such dreadful, horrific, appalling and revolting scene churned our guts. The scene was a straight lift from Bhairav Chatti. His avatar is frightening and wrathful. Shivji is also known as the Master of Ghost, the Protector of Ghost and the Moon Carrier. He gave us the taste of all the three in a single night. As Bhairav spread terror, Shivji was not far behind. I am unable to describe the dreadful scene of Bhairav. He shivered and we would pull over the bed sheet in fear!

People were annoyed, irritated and tired. With insects making strange noises and horses neighing around us, we were tired but unable to sleep. As usual it was so dark that we could not see who was sleeping next to us. At around 2.30 am, we heard a lady screaming out loudly. The sudden scream in the deserted and desolate atmosphere was frightening. The sound was emitted just once, but the effect was so horrific that none of us could sleep thereafter. It was really daunting and gruesome. Shivji has made us experience all His three swaroops in those few days. We all were numbed by the noise. None of us had an iota of strength to speak out a single word.

Life Struggle, Day-3

JUNE 21, 2013 DAY 17

The day started as usual. We woke up with the sun rising. We had acclimatised ourselves to the situation and conditions. We were eagerly waiting for the military to reach and rescue us. However as the day progressed, hope and enthusiasm started to ebb.

The first thing we asked was, "Did you hear the scream last night?" All of us had heard the piercing scream. It had become a subject of hot discussion. It was still echoing in our ears. The subject of military arrival was replaced by the topic of the scream of last night. Everyone was frightened and the fear was palpable. It was the town of God of Ghost. Shivji is Bhuteshwar. People believed that the souls of pilgrims who had lost their lives here in the last three to four days were roaming around and making freaky voices in the night. It was really nerve-wracking.

The Uncle who had provided me with the ointment wanted me to apply it again. He remarked that he had lost his family - daughter, son-in-law and his wife! He was worried about his future. There were some in his group who did not know the fate of their relatives.

Dayanand said, "I had a group of tourists with me. We were stationed at Rambada. I just came down to check the condition of the road but could not return. I heard that Rambada has been wiped off I am worried about the fate of the 20 people, who were with me. I don't know why I decided to come down leaving them alone! I never leave my groups alone. Who made me take the decision is beyond my imagination!"

In the meantime Jharkhand Uncle, his wife along with some others excitedly remarked, "Enough is enough! I cannot take it anymore. Days will just pass by if we do not act. Nobody is going to help. We are going to climb the mountain." He did not budge from his stance in spite of our reasoning with him. They left soon after. There was perceptibly less crowd now. Dayanand said, "I would also have gone long ago." However he was deterred by the jungle route and now he felt helpless.

Today the first call was from home. Jasmina ran to take the call. A boy stopped her in her tracks offering a biscuit, "*Ye lo Didi, biscuit kha lo.*" (Take a biscuit didi.) She was extremely surprised and remarked "*Nahi aap khaalo.*" (No dear, you eat it.) The boy replied, "*Nahi pura din bhaagte ho to khaana to chaahiye na.*" (As you are running about the whole day you need to eat.) She said, "*Mere badle aap khaalo.*" (You eat it instead.) But he would not listen. Boy's father was listening to their conversation. He came from behind and advised Jasmina to eat so that the boy would be happy.

Jasmina was really putting in lot of efforts in attending calls and sharing the plans. Jasmina had to go up and down to attend the calls from our family members back home. It is all the more difficult when you are hungry. We were exhausted. Everyone was waiting to be evacuated.

Our rescue operation was getting delayed. Choppers would come and throw the parcels of food and medicines. Due to the slope and undulating hills, the parcel would roll over into the river. Out of 100 packets, only 20 would land on the ground and the rest would go down straight in the river. Today we did not go to pick the packets as we had no strength left in us. Shilpaben had told us that this time they were arranging for blankets, medicine and batteries.

Taneja Uncle's cell phone's battery was getting low and he advised us to talk for the last time, which worried us a lot. Jasmina thought of a plan: We pick up the parcels which were stuck in the trees. She approached Taneja Uncle and explained the plan to him. Uncle went up the slope and convinced a man to extricate the bags. He sportingly offered him food packets for his family as we needed the batteries from the packets. The man got convinced. They opened up a doli and got a thick rope and a bamboo. They tied one end of the rope to the railing and other to the man's waist. He went down in the valley and extricated the parcels from the tree. The man took the challenge for the sake of his family and had the pleasure of getting food for them. Unfortunately there were no batteries. Presently another chopper fluttered in. This time they were throwing blankets. We did not get any, but one group ahead of us caught four of them. Jasmina requested that it was our family who was sending the blankets. The man agreed and handed over two blankets to her.

Slowly the crowd started to disperse. Dayanand went up to investigate. Our family and relatives were putting in their best efforts for us. Chintu Jijaji in the US prepared the map of Kedarnath finding our location. They contacted top TV News channels and senior military personnel soliciting their help to reach us. They also appointed private professional Dolphine trekkers from Dehradun who could bring the essential supplies and medicines for us. Further they had made arrangement for choppers. Within three days, 1,000 of calls and many vows were made in various temples for our safe return. All our brothers Mama and Masa in Dehradun were ready in attendance, doing their best to extricate us from the impossible situation. Shilpaben was relaying all the messages, even some of the inconsequential ones, which were very reassuring for our morale. She informed us that military personnel were preparing a helipad at Jungle Chatti but not to move as trekkers will guide us there.

In Guptakashi, the whole day Prince and Nishant were collating information of Operation Rescue from both sides. Cars were requisitioned in advance so that no time was lost once we landed. They visited all the six helipads and got all our names registered. This will help Prince know from where we had arrived. Arrangements were in place in case we had to be shifted from one helipad to another. In the worst case, we may have to stay overnight so he arranged a hotel room for night stay.

Earlier we heard from Shilpaben that military men were building a helipad in Jungle Chatti. Around 4 that evening, Dayanand told us that a helipad was under construction and everyone has started moving towards Jungle Chatti. Now we were in two minds - whether to go up or stay put. Kaka was not able to walk. Aunty was also not well and I was injured. Shilpaben had asked us to stay where we were. She had told us that private trekkers were on the way and they could reach us any moment. If we moved they would not be able to track us. I told Dayanand to wait for a while as we had to discuss and decide. He declined. He could not wait anymore; he was becoming restless as there was no food and water for the past few days. He reluctantly said that he was going up. At the turn he felt reluctant to leave us. He was in two minds and was not able to decide. He left us and I got scared.

Taneja Uncle informed us to talk with Shilpaben. Jasmina was very tired; her legs gave up as she was shivering. She asked Bini to go up and speak with Shilpaben. Bini declined as it was too dirty; she could not walk. Finally I went up and spoke with Shilpaben. I told her that people have started moving uphill towards Jungle Chatti. What should we do? She told us to wait a while; she will call us back. She called up again and confirmed the news of a new helipad being constructed at Jungle Chatti.

Hearing it Kaka could not contain himself. He was very angry and said that if they can help us, it is okay, else leave us to our fate. For three days we had been hearing the same story. "As the phone batteries will die soon, leave us alone to die," he told me to convey it to Shilpaben.

Bharti called me. My eyes filled with tears as I told her everything Kaka told me. I could make out from her voice that she was also crying. "Ektaa please listen patiently, nothing is in our hands. We could not do anything even after trying our best. Do what military people are telling you to. They will be able to rescue you, so just go uphill."

I relayed the message from Bharti to everyone. On the basis of her guidance we were trying to muster courage to walk the distance. We started moving up. After 15 minutes Shilpaben also told us to start moving up along with the other group; not to remain alone.

My legs were hurting. My shoes were torn. I had to walk bare feet. But Jasmina did not allow me to do that and gave me her shoes with a hard look that deterred me from arguing. She walked bare feet. It was a really difficult task. We had to cross the three mountains that we had overcome a few days ago. We had to leave the heavy blankets behind.

I requested Taneja Uncle to support Aunty while climbing up as she had weakened considerably. I was worried for Kaka as he too was weak by now and could not walk at all. But he showed the guts and started walking without cribbing. Lilaba and Mom too showed courage and will-power and started climbing. By now the rivulets had started drying up. We had to cross all the waterfalls and landslides again till Jungle Chatti. The muddy landslides were drying up by now; the waterfall had lost its force to a great extent. Mandakini was still flowing in her own inimitable style. Roads were still slippery and difficult to climb. As we were crossing we got the news that one chopper had crashed while taking off; the blades clashed with nearby mountain slopes. Luckily there were no casualties. So the rescue operation had been stopped immediately; there will be no more rescue for the day. We were dejected. We understood that it will be one more night in Jungle Chatti. We were feeling depressed. Military would search for another place. They will have to level the mountain for the helipad, which may take up a day or two.

On the way we came across a Gujarati family who were preparing Khichadi for dinner. They offered us some; we declined as I was not sure of the water they had used to make the khichadi. Uncle got lured by it and swiftly decided to stay the night there as he saw good arrangements for food. Taneja Uncle came down and said we should continue moving and find some place with better shelter. We agreed. Uncle asked the Gujaratis if they had anything to eat. Rice was over but they still had some potatoes and onions, which they offered to him. Uncle got excited with the prospect and switched the gas on. He called one boy, offered him some money and asked him to bring water from the waterfall. We all were shocked to see Uncle's behaviour. The boy smiled, "By God's grace I have enough money so I do not need any, but all the same I will help you." Uncle was flummoxed. Aunty looking at Kaka nervously and remarked, "Rajnibhai, his behaviour is directly related to his hunger. Let us move from here." Uncle actually took a potato and an onion for emergency.

We learnt a lesson. When you are in urgent need of money, even people with deep pockets or excessive love for money may not come forward to help you. Only your good behaviour and good deeds help you out. At the moment money had no value; it was just a piece of paper. Your aim for life should be good behaviour and an attitude to help and sacrifice all the way. Money is necessary but is not the Ultimate. When you reach the kingdom of god, money loses its importance. It is certain that from here on, the accounts of your behaviour and deeds will decide whether the doors of Heaven or Hell will open for you.

On reaching the new place, we felt happy and refreshed. It was a clear road on one side of the mountain and a big valleyon the other side, with Mandakini River flowing. The earlier place was completely littered and dirty. Those who had drunk the water were suffering from dysentery and old people had become weak. There had been more bodies than living ones. Here it was colder than expected as there was no protection from the trees. We looked for a shelter to protect us from still randomly falling stones.

People had reached Jungle Chatti but we were standing midway as no one knew where the new helipad will be constructed.

We told Taneja Uncle that we were not used to extreme cold. He said not to worry. He went down again and brought one big plastic and few more plastics to be used as blankets. As we were 16 people (with Taneja Uncle's family) we decided to cut them into four equal pieces. The plan was to accommodate four people in a row; accordingly four such rows were placed in parallel. Uncle came looking for the blanket. Bini asked him to be patient as we were trying to accommodate everyone. That triggered Uncle's anger due to hunger; he vented his ire on Bini, but took my name, which triggered an argument.

Taneja Uncle bought sugar and tea from a shanty , which people had already looted. He lit a bonfire with the wood, made black tea and offered it to us. When we declined he insisted we should have one to fight the cold. Each could just take one sip.

It was dark now. Peace prevailed. At around 10 pm, military men came up and spoke to us. Everyone heaved a sigh of relief and was delighted. They talked with every group. They told Mom, "You all will be rescued tomorrow and this is your last night here. Now that we are here, do not worry. If you have any problems, call us." I asked the military man as to why they took so many days to reach us. He explained that due to extensive damage, it was impossible to reach up to this point. They had to take the jungle route to reach here.

That entire night I could not sleep as Aunty crawled involuntarily towards Bini and me. I gave away my place to Bini. I was left with no place to sleep and sat up the whole night. We shook Aunty to shift a little but she was fast asleep. Flowing river and the open area made the weather freezing cold. I was shivering like a leaf. The night was very miserable for me. I was repeatedly talking with Bini and asking her, "Are you sleeping Bini? How much will you sleep?" After some time she stopped replying. She slept peacefully. During night I got up to attend nature's call. Mom stopped me enquiring where I was going. I told her I need to go to the restroom. She said, "Wait, don't go alone; take Kaka along." Kaka came with me. As I was about to wear my shoes, I saw one potato and one onion resting in Uncle's shoes. I laughed aloud and could not stop!

Krishnaji has elaborated the principles of work: Do your work; do not expect the fruit. Depending upon your deeds you shall achieve. Though we read it daily, today it was a revelation. Kaka gifted two blankets; he got to use two blankets. However, those had to be left behind. Our hard earned money was of no use to us. It is said you cannot get before your time nor will you get more than is destined. This maxim aptly describes the situation we were in. We left many things behind thinking they were of no use. Those who remained were destined to use them. Circumstances conspired in such a way that our things passed on to them. If we compare our lows and highs with Gitaji we easily get our answers we are seeking. We learnt a lesson in Kalyug period that man is a selfish being. He remembers all his deeds but tends to forget the people who obliged him. "I did but he did not reciprocate." He would rather complain about people not reciprocating his good deeds, coolly forgetting that he did not either. This could be a salient feature of the Kalyug era.

Do not yearn for Heaven. Do not fear Hell. No one knows what is sin or virtue. Just ensure that your deeds do not hurt anyone. Rest, leave it to Him.

Operation Rescue Day

JUNE 22, 2013 DAY 18

At about 4, the sun rose. The day brought hope as we were to be let out from here. A wave of happiness surged through us; there was a spring in our steps.

Bini was enjoying a nice sleep, sleeping as if on a soft mattress with still softer quilt at home. She quickly removed the plastic from her face and stared at me. I was looking at her expressionlessly. I blurted out, "Were you sleeping at home?" She just laughed.

Our happy days were here again. It was time to relax as at around 5, our privately hired trekkers finally traced us. They had undertaken a grave risk by opting for the jungle route to reach us. Prince and Nishant had given up at Guptakashi for lack of courage and experience. We felt immense relief. Without a moment's rest they tended to our needs. Firstly the trekkers gave essential medicine of blood pressure and diabetes to Aunty, Mom and Lilaba. They raised tents for us. They applied some anti-bacterial medicines on our wounds. They also rustled up Maggie for us on a portable stove. As we had one spoon of it, Jasmina felt like vomiting due to fasting for so many days. Trekkers were carrying cell phones with them, so we spoke with Bhaveshbhai, Jijaji and others. Dr Kamleshbhai from Ahmedabad advised us not to have any solid food. Instead he asked us to have Maggie soup. The trekkers lugged loads of luggage for us while coming up, whereas we could not carry even two blankets!

The trekkers were well equipped. After many days we got to brush our teeth. We relaxed in the tent. We could see the rescue team and military men working hard to construct the helipad. They had selected one turning point as a place for makeshift helipad. They had levelled the mountain and uprooted the railing from the corner ensuring there was no repeat of the last mishap. It was a risky landing for the pilots. First they did a trial with four-seater chopper followed by seven-seater and then 10. They were successful in all of them.

Within half an hour our trekkers told us to stand in queue. Luckily it was hardly 100 metres away from where we were sitting. We stood in the queue, which had just started forming. There must have been around 20-25 people standing ahead of us. Initially we were being informed by the military that rescue will be effected family-wise. We thought it would be good as all eight would be accommodated in one chopper. Their plan changed. They now had a priority list according to which the first preference will be given to those who were injured, followed by old people, women and children and finally men and young boys. They had created barriers of bamboos from where the queue started. Ahead of the barriers the soldiers adviced us to form group of eight so that as soon as the aircraft landed this group could board the aircratt. Shilpaben advised us to alight at Phata helipad at Guptakashi where Prince would be waiting to receive us.

Uncle told Kaka, "Let Aunty go first as she is injured and is a woman; she should get priority." Considering the hardship we had undergone, Kaka felt we should stay together. We told Uncle to remain together and move along. But Uncle declined and told Kaka, "I must be allowed to do things in my own way, Rajnibhai." Kaka said, "Okay, you go ahead with your plans." We were a bit disappointed. Maybe he was worrying about Aunty and his hunger! Uncle informed the jawan about Aunty's health.

Those who climbed Jungle Chatti had queued up on the other side of the slope. When the copter landed, it raised a fair amount of dust. You may get thrown up along with air if you were too close. Hence jawans guided us by holding our hands. The chopper service got regularised. Aunty got a chance to board the copter early. Uncle, who got left out the first time, was accommodated in the next service. He could not even bid us good bye; maybe he was very tense.

Aunty alighted at one of the six helipads in Guptakashi (medical camp). While Uncle at Phata helipad! He started searching for her.

Now the crowd was increasing. Stranded people had started gathering like honey bees. They were thronging around the rescue point. Slowly the crowd was becoming uncontrollable. People were pulling at one another and shouting at each other. The conditions were ripe for a stampede. Military men were requesting each and every one to be calm and to sit down. No one was paying attention to their request. People were scared as no one wanted to spend another night in such a situation in spite of the assurance that they will be rescued that day itself. People were mobbing each other. We were fearful that the condition could get worse any moment.

As we were struggling to stay in the line, Aunty was rushed to the medical camp to monitor her sugar level and the attendant weakness. Unaware, Uncle was enquiring frantically with the jawans about Aunty.

As I was standing in the queue a lady put her weight on me, which was very irritating. I told her very politely to stand straight as we were tired and injured. She would not listen. After requesting her politely thrice, I lost my temper and yelled. Kaka could not stand any longer as the pain had increased. He was supporting himself against the slope. We were pushed by south Indian men, who were standing next to us and wanted to jump the queue. They were pushing Mom and Lilaba very hard, who requested them to stand properly and not to push them. They would not listen or understand our language. Suddenly one of the men from the group pressed my right toe with immense force. I shrieked with pain and was down to tears. It pained a lot. I just could not withstand the pain standing in the queue. A man from the rescue team saw me crying in pain. He quickly made some space for me to sit. I managed to make some more space for Kaka to sit as his legs were also paining.

Lilaba and Mom's turn came up earlier due to their age and were lifted to Gaurikund. It seemed a tough task to get rescued today. We were worried that our turn may not come today. The pain was increasing all over again. The person who offered me a seat advised us, "Keep moving ahead slowly or else we will be left here." He was right. The line started moving. Presently Kaka and I managed to reach the starting point. Jasmina and Bini managed to get place to seat. Our turn came up. I requested military men to allow Kaka to come along with me as we both were injured. They assured me that they will allow Kaka to accompany me. The chopper arrived. However as my turn came a Jawan quickly held my hand and pulled me in the chopper leaving Kaka behind. Tears welled up. I looked at Kaka and our eyes met. His eyes silently beseeched me to go ahead. I was reluctant to leave him behind, but it was not in my hands. They just shoved me in the chopper.

Now Kaka, Jasmina and Bini were left behind.

Uncle got to know that Aunty was in the medical camp; he hired a taxi to be with her. Mom and Lilaba were waiting for us in Gaurikund.

My chopper took flight. I was always fascinated by the chopper and wanted to fly in it. It was 12-seater chopper; I was the last one to get in. It was very noisy inside the chopper. My seat was at the tail end meant for the luggage. It was very suffocating. I kept my head down and prayed for it to land fast. There were six to seven people on the chairs. One sick lady seemed unconscious. I thought it would hardly take 10 minutes for a chopper to cover the distance to Gaurikund as it was hardly 2.5 km from the rescue point. It took half an hour. The air was thin and the chopper was hot like a steam engine and stifling.

An aged man spoke to me but I was not able to hear him. I asked him to be quiet. He came closer to me, smiled and told me, "*Meri biwi gayi.*" (My wife gone.) I did not understand what he wanted to convey. Whether that he had lost his wife or she had been rescued. I just ignored him and asked him to be quiet.

After half an hour the chopper landed. As I was sitting last I did not know where we had landed. I was feeling totally blank and overwhelmed. All the initial exuberance had vanished. As I came down I saw a mass of media reporters and medical camp attendants. Military personnel came running towards us and started enquiring about our health. They took us to the Medical Camp. *Do you have any injury? Any problems? How is your health?* I was given first-aid treatment. My wounds were cleaned; Band-Aid rolled round my toe. I was given some vitamin tablets. A few officers were noting down our contact numbers; they enquired about the number of family members with us and their wellbeing. They directed me to a seat in a room.

I walked down the building. Many people had organised free meals and fruit juice for the rescued people. They were serving with love and encouraging us to have more. I humbly refused to have anything as I was not feeling up to it. However, I accepted only a small juice bottle and kept it in my bag. I just wanted to meet my family members. They had made arrangements for a bath.

Above Jasmina, Bini and Kaka's turn had arrived. Dusk was upon us. They could have completed five more sorties. Bini was guiding Kaka. Our family members were coaxing and applying pressure so that all the others also would be rescued. As rain was forecast for the next day, young and healthy people guided by the jawans had started climbing down. As Dayanand was also walking, he asked them to follow him. Bini and Jasmina were asked to walk. But they refused summarily and rebuked the jawans, "It is ridiculous to suggest the girls to walk on such a treacherous road. My entire family is rescued." They were sent by chopper service.

When the chopper arrived, three people got up. Someone hit Bini's hand, forcing her to release Kaka's hand and hold someone else's hand. Jawan guided them inside. They realised that Kaka was left out. They got worried as he is reticent and does not speak up. Further he also could not speak due to a swollen vocal cord.

Here in Guptakashi Uncle could meet Aunty. The taxi fellow refused money as the government was offering free service..

I was perplexed. I was eagerly waiting for our family members to arrive. I got up and had a word with the military personnel in Gochar.

Officer: Where do you want to go..?

I: I am waiting for my family members to come. My Mom and Aunty were rescued before me; where can I find them?

Officer: You don't worry. They must be safe. There are totally six helipads, so they must be in one of them. But where do you want to go...?

I: Could I get a cell phone for a minute? I want to talk to my family.

I was alone. No one knew about my whereabouts. They were searching frantically for me.

He stared at me.

Officer: Ya, ya madam, why not?

He was shy and reluctant to give his cell phone as his phone had a wallpaper of a model.

I called Shilpaben. Before I asked her anything, she started saying...

Shilpaben: Where are you? We all are worried about you.

I: I'm alone. I'm waiting for Kaka, Jasmina and Bini to come. Now, where do I have to go?

Shilpaben: Jasmina and Bini have reached Gaurikund. Their chopper was going to Phata. When they saw Mom and Lilaba, they got down. No idea about Kaka. Where are you now...?

I asked the military man.

Officer: Gochar...!

I: (over the phone) I'm at Gochar Airbase.

Shilpaben: Ok wait. Note down the number I am giving you now and call him. Do not move anywhere; Prince is coming to pick you up.

I: I don't have anything to write. You ask him to call me on this number.

Shilpaben: OK. But, you don't go anywhere.

Call over.

Prince was waiting at Phata. Jasmina and Bini were searching for a chopper to go to Phata. Jawans were not ready for it. Lilaba gave in; she could not help crying. Jawans, realising the gravity of the situation, allowed them entry. Now Jasmina and Bini were left out; were being forced to walk down. They informed Shilpaben who in turn talked to Prince, who turned her suggestion down saying the roads are very bad. Now they were trying to go to Phata.

After 10 minutes....the officer came running towards me.

Officer: There was a call from your sister. Someone is coming to pick you up from here.

After some time another jawan informed me about washroom facalities created for pilgrims..

I: Thanks. I'm fine.

Meantime, a reporter from India TV news channel approached me for an interview. I asked him to do me favour and lend me his cell phone so that I could make a call to Shilpaben; this time Bharti was on the call. Shilpaben and Bharti were fighting with each other and were not listening to what I wanted to say. They were discussing about me; where to send and how to send.

Nikhil Jijaji called me.

Nikhil Jijaji: Ektaa, is there any place where you can stay tonight...? Any good family with you...?

(I was shocked to hear that. I looked around hurriedly.)

I: No Jijaji, I cannot stay here. No place to stay. I do not want to spend a night here.

Kaka was waiting for chopper at Jungle Chatti. Fortunately he got into the last chopper service which took him to Gochar. He also felt choked like me. He requested, "*Niche utaaro nahi to mar jaaunga.*" (Get me out of here I am not able to breath or I will die) and he started losing consciousness. After reaching Gochar,jawans lifted him and took him to the medical camp where he was immediately put on oxygen.(I was not aware of this.)

In Gaurikund, Bini started crying inconsolably as she was scared. A Jawan, sympathising with her, informed her that he will make arrangements to take her to Phata. PG Uncle and Aunty, who were in touch with the family had reached Phata. Mom and Lilaba were waiting for Jasmina and Bini to arrive. A Jawan stepped in and told them to be comfortable in a bus meant to drop them at their destination.

Ba: (they refused) We are waiting for our daughters to come.

Jawan: They will also have to come to the bus. You proceed.

Ba and Mom went to the bus, which was vacant except for the driver.

Thereafter, Padmanabhbhai called me...

Padmanabhbhai: Ektaa, cry. Cry loudly and say you want to go to Dehradun. You have to somehow come to Dehradun.

I wondered why I was being told to cry.

Military people in Gochar enquired where I wanted to go; they were ready to make arrangements to drop me as well. My family members were asking me to stay there. I could not understand why they were telling me to cry.

As I ended the call, I saw Dayanand's wife (didi). I was delighted to see her. She had come with Mom and Ba in the chopper from Jungle Chatti. I thought that Ba and Mom must also be here. I went to her and asked about them.

Didi: They are at Gaurikund. What are you doing here?

I: I'm waiting for Kaka.

Didi: He's already here in Gochar.

I: Are you sure...?

Didi: Yep I saw him. Military men carried him on their shoulders out of the chopper.

I got worried for Kaka. I was tense as to why they had to carry Kaka on the shoulder. . I realised that he was not able to walk. My mind stopped working.

After repeated requests,military people accommodated Jasmina and Bini in a chopper that was going to Phata helipad.

When Kaka did not turn up, I got really anxious. Leaving my bag, I ran and bumped into the same reporter whom I had met earlier.

Reporter: You wanted to go to Dehradun, right?

I nodded.

Reporter: There is Captain Soni here who is going to Dehradun. If you want you can go along with him. Or else you have to wait for the bus, which will take 12 hours of bumpy ride to Dehradun.

I ran back to collect my bag and rushed to the medical camp. Kaka was sleeping on a mattress with an oxygen mask on his face. I was stunned and asked him anxiously. "Kaka, all well?"

Kaka: (he whispered) I was unconscious. They lifted me to put me on oxygen.

I: How are you feeling?

Kaka nodded, indicating he is better.

I: Can you walk?

Kaka nodded. I offered my hand for him to get up.

I: Come on we need to go now.

Kaka: Where do we have to go?

I. Do not ask anything now. Let's move out of here.

We looked for a chopper going to Dehradun.

The moment Bini and Jasmina landed at Phata they started searching for Mom and Lilaba. They saw them in the bus. They also boarded the bus. They were unaware where the bus was heading for. As the bus started, there was an announcement asking for Patels. It was Prince. Immediately Bini, Ba, Jasmina, and Mom shouted out in chorus.

Prince banged on the bus to halt and got them out of the bus. They left for the hotel in Guptakashi in a jeep. Now the only task left was to search for Aunty and Uncle?

While Kaka and I were looking for some means to reach Dehradun, a reporter approached us for an interview. I restrained Kaka from giving one as we had to leave this place first and fast. We saw a military chopper parked. It was carrying fuel from Gochar to Dehradun. We got into it. There were big tins of aluminium filled with fuel and the smell pervaded the aircraft. There were many small circular windows. There were many who wanted to go to Dehradun. Many people started closing the windows the moment chopper started flying. The officer said to keep them open. It was very suffocating inside even here. We were reaching closer to our family members. Heart was a bag of mixed emotions. I did not know how I would react when I would see my family. I anticipated the moment with excitement. It took around 30 minutes to reach Dehradun. We were dropped in the middle of the runway. The officers asked us to move off the runway fast.

As I came out of the chopper, I just sat down on the runway itself. I was feeling very uneasy and dehydrated. I was feeling short of oxygen. Kaka was shocked to see me in such a condition. I still had the juice bottle with me. I had a sip. I felt a little better. I stood up and told Kaka, "Do not worry. I am fine now." People were running off the runway from the swirl of air of the chopper. As I looked back, a south Indian man was running struggling to hold his lungi in place as it was flying. I turned my face away.

An ambulance came and shifted us from the runway. Government officers enquired about the whereabouts of our family, so that they could drop us with them. I felt like I was in a new world. Everything was new to me. My conscience was like a new slate. I said carelessly I did not know! I called Shilpaben and informed her that we had landed in Dehradun waiting for further instructions. Without listening she asked me to jot down one number. I replied that it was not possible to note down any number as I did not have a pen or paper to write. I just handed over the phone to a man from the government office asking Shilpaben to explain to him. We called Padmanabhbhai and he gave him directions to reach him at Jolly Grand Airport.

At one point we were stopped and asked for all the details pertaining to Operation Rescue. We furnished all the details and completed the formalities. Many people got down here. We were shifted to another ambulance. Every single second weighed on us. As the bus moved there was a vortex of emotions increasing my heart beats. We were impatient to meet our family members.

Finally as ambulance was passing through the narrow lane of the restricted area, we saw a blue door at the exit point. The escort opened the door and I felt like a newly born. There was a sea of humanity surrounding the ambulance. In each heart arose a spring of hope and suspense whose relatives would alight first, whether their relatives were present. People peeped through the windows as it came to a halt. They started banging on the ambulance. Din and bustle. We were apprehensive and felt numb; uncertainty gave way to a low feeling. The events of last few days made the noise demoralising.

We saw Ketanbhai, son of PG Uncle, and Nimishbhai from Sydney, my cousin, in the crowd. Eyes met. The 'frozen' heart began melting. The body became cold; hands and legs weakened. They started banging on the ambulance shouting, "They are our family, stop the ambulance." The driver stopped the ambulance. We were so eager to meet our family that even an innocuous door seemed like a mountain!

I was at the door. Nimeshbhai and I tried to touch hands through the glass window. He has always protected me and I have always felt secure with him. The moment the door opened, he lifted me in his arms, planting a kiss on my forehead and patted me. I felt relieved as I tried to hold back my tears. But I couldn't and broke down. All emotions surged out. Kaka was still inside the ambulance, Nimishbhai went up to him and hugged him; he started crying. The moment was electric, sentimental and effusive. I was feeling speechless. Tears welled up in my eyes. Ketanbhai helped me to a chair. Padmanabhbhai came running and hugged me and I started crying. He told me to relax as we were here, everything will be fine. I was feeling very much relaxed, protected, secure and assured after meeting them. I felt a strange warmth take over me on meeting my family. Strangers gathered round me and started showing me the photographs of their loved ones, whether we had seen them. They did not know whether their relatives were alive or not. Some of the bodies were mutilated beyond recognition so in some cases photographs may not help. Some families were fortunate to be united while some members had got separated from their loved ones. For some of them it was the curse of Shivji, and for some, blessing. Those who realised it took it as a lesson while some were left cursing Shivji's Tandav.

In Guptakashi Jasmina, Bini, Lilaba and Mom were accommodated by Prince and Nishant in a small local house which was converted into a hotel and left in search for PG Uncle and Aunty who had reached Guptakashi from the medical camp. Within half an hour they zeroed in on them and took them to the hotel.

At the airport I met Nikhil Jijaji. He hugged me and kissed my forehead. He congratulated me and said, "Eku you have done it. Eku you are the champ." I was feeling blessed to have such a wonderful family. I exhorted God to inspire me to continue doing good deeds in future.

We directly went to the hospital. They put us on saline.

Our hotel in Dehradun was one and half hour drive from Jolly Grant Airport. No one uttered a word. It was time to enjoy but it did not sink in yet as the scars that were inflicted during the ordeal were still raw and fresh and may not heal in a hurry.

The hotel in Guptakashi, where Jasmina and others were, was short on basic amenities. Before the calamity, Gaurikund would be abuzz with activities 24x7. Today all houses were grounded. Prince somehow procured hot water – for seven days we had not seen hot water! Shivji, in whose fun and frolic gave the opportunity to experience the life of Aghoribaba. which ultimately proved to be very tough and fatal to many. Aghoris are ascetic Shaiva sadhus with ashes smeared on their bodies. We also passed through the test but were left with deep scars.

Prince massaged warm oil into Lilaba and Mom's soles, which relaxed the frozen muscles. He arranged home-made food with great difficulty. Not everyone gets an opportunity to serve. You just need to care for the welfare of others and opportunity presents itself.

At night we reached our hotel in Dehradun. We had food today. After seven long days we saw a plate of rice and a bowl of daal. We realised the importance of water. However, as the grain of rice passed through the food pipe, it sort of bounced back like a ball as we had no food for the last seven days. The stomach was not used to it since a week. Just had a little of it and that was it. The soft mattresses were like soft gold after spending restless nights on the uneven surface for seven days. At the end, due to God's grace, we came out and left behind the troubled times. The reasoning power had not yet returned. We felt as if the world has stopped. We were not able to enjoy our release. Images of dead bodies were streaming in front of our eyes. We could not help thinking about the people who were still stranded and still trying to escape. We had undergone the life's ups and downs in seven days. How did we come here? All was a blur, a dream, an illusion, a phantasm! Did we come or were we pushed here. Did we get saved by our decisions or who inspired us to take the decisions? Today we shall be sleeping under the cover of love of our family.

A relative of the Gujarati family who offered us khichadi informed us that one of their members had died by having the khichadi. This made us realise that at every step we were guided by God to take the right decisions. He made us take the decision to leave Rambada in spite of having all the facilities, for Jungle Chatti. If we had stayed overnight at Rambada, we would have been swept away like others.

The moment we reached the plains people from different states were providing help to their respective people. It saddened us. Every person and their lives from all states are equally important. We still find lack of unity even after Independence. Instead of restricting ourselves to our state we should go all out to help all the people irrespective of which state they hail from. This would have avoided the death caused due to shortage of food and medicine supplies. The government of Maharastra had deputed some senior officials at the collector level for the rescue operation, who were stationed at Dehradun. One of them was Shri Rajendra Madhne, populerly known as Bapu Sahib. He came to meet us at our hotel in Deheradun and inquired about our health and ask if we needed any kind of help. We were very happy to meet him.

Struggle in Dehradun

JUNE 23, 2013 DAY 19

Today Kaka and I wanted to enjoy sleep; sound and deep. However Ba, Jasmina, Bini, Mom, Aunty and Uncle were stranded in Phata. They had to come to Dehradun. Prince woke them up at 3 am. None of them had the strength to even open their eyes. They forced themselves to wake up. They were to come to Dehradun by chopper. They had to go to Phata helipad as the roads had given way. The weather worsened. As clouds gathered the chopper hired by us could not fly. They waited in the shed for more than an hour but to no avail. Prince and Nishant were running around looking for choppers.

When they came to know that Operation Rescue had started at Guptakashi as weather improved they rushed there. No choppers were going to Dehradun. Prince and Nishant enlisted the help of Jawans, but to no avail. Two hours went by. Hopes were giving way to despair. They were snatching their 40 winks. They could not think coherently as they were in the grip of sleep.

Three hours elapsed but no result. It was 11 am and still no signs of chopper.

Here we were in the same boat. We were waiting for them to land here. A hired plane was parked waiting for us to fly to Mumbai. They made us wait. Again we had a nap. We could hardly eat anything for breakfast.

There Nishant learnt that a chopper was going to Dehradun. He ran to call them. Prince had left his walkie talkie with Bini. In the mean time airforce officer came and informed them that chopper is ready for take off to Dehradun. They all rushed and boarded the aircraft. Seeing this, Prince also rushed and somehow boarded the same aircraft. Everyone assembled and got into the chopper. Everyone heaved a sigh of relief.

However, remembering the sufferings at the medical camp made us cry. Many diabetics suffered from decomposing legs; many had fracture and many were unconscious.

God's ways are inscrutable. Those who had yet to complete their karma-chakras,in spite of injuries, sufferings and various wounds, could come down and lead a normal life.. Those who completed their karma-chakras, inspite of their good health they died. The pilgrims did not suffer till they were at any of the Char Dhams. The moment they left the Dham they suffered from dysentery and some lost their voices. A few fell unconscious due to weakness and many could not walk due to freezing. In spite of so many difficulties, in the Dhams, their health was good. It was due to the air touched by the Shivji and his fragrance that protected the pilgrims from the diseases.

At Gupakashi Ba, Jasmina, Bini, Mom, Aunty and Uncle got the chopper used by the military for dropping boxes and alighting at inaccessible places. Its rear was open to the sky. They were sitting closely entwining their hands and fingers lest they slide down! The beauty outside was breath-taking but the destruction was appalling. Green leaves had turned ashen. Mountains had a layered look, trees and clearings alternating. Many got down at Gochar. Those who headed for Dehradun were to alight at Gochar and then board it again.

Kaka and I were tired waiting at the hotel. My world had got stalled. Everything was moving around but we were still stunned. We went upstairs to sleep. Last night I slept as if in a trance; I was in another world. I felt as if I had no existence. It was surely the deepest and longest sleep I had. I slept like a child nonchalantly. As we had been in God's lap the meditative state induced deep sleep in us.

Ba, Jasmina, Bini, Mom, Aunty and Uncle, after waiting for another hour, were told that there was no chopper service to Dehradun. Further they were told to go by bus, which would take 12 hours. This was exasperating as nobody was in a condition to travel by bus. Prince and Nishant were exploring other possibilities of getting a chopper for Dehradun. Seeing their efforts going in vain, Jasmina got annoyed with the military officer and tried to approach the rescue-in-charge at Gochar. She asked a military officer about the in-charge; they declined to give any information. Jasmina started shouting loudly in front of the media persons. The military official sheepishly requested her to calm down, promising to arrange something soon. Within 30 minutes a military officer informed them that a chopper was waiting to go to Dehradun. The mood turned jubilant and they ran towards the chopper as fast as they could. After half an hour the chopper landed at Dehradun.

Malti Aunty had weakened considerably. She was taken to the Jolly Grant Hospital on a stretcher. She was given treatment. The jawans requested everyone to clear the area around the hospital.

Heart beat away apprehensively. There were tears of happiness around. We were confounded and confused. Padmanabhbhai, Nimeshbhai, Ketanbhai and Jijaji were waiting for them. There was much hugging and crying. Ultimately all efforts put in were delivering excellent results, which received an all-round seal of approval. The moment was very important and sensitive for our families and friends. Ultimately we were together safely.

We were not able to react to the enthusiastic and happy surroundings. Signs of fatigue surfaced. There was an atmosphere of Diwali in the family as if we were returning after an exile (vanwas) of 14 years. However it troubled and haunted me that there were thousands of families who were still searching helplessly for their lost dear ones. Many were being extricated from the rubble of the dilapidated and razed houses. Havoc and destruction were extensive and widespread as villages after villages were inundated and swept away mercilessly. We immediately retired to our rooms.

One thing was certain, our ultimate goal was to reach Mumbai safely. Like Arjun (aiming at the eye of bird) we had only one objective and we were thinking about the same all the time. Due to this sole objective all our efforts were directed in the same direction and hence we could achieve our goal. I learnt a big lesson - if we channelise our energies in accomplishing our goal, we can definitely achive it, in spite of various difficulties on the way. Only self-assurance is required. Only one question, one answer. The math will definitely work.

Dehradun to Ahmedabad

JUNE 24, 2013 DAY 20

Everything around us felt new as we tried to reconcile a world of death and destruction to a world of dreams and development. We stood rooted while the world passed by. We were ready to mould our brand new world leaving the past behind. Memories of our baptism by fire and the lessons and experiences gained thereof were truly and permanently etched in our psyche forever. We need to concentrate on the new opportunities coming our way rather than rue the past. Our conscience had become pure and sublime. Our attitude changed for the better and acquired the intrinsic energy to fight our inner foes. All negative emotions like envy, ego, deceit and grief will be left behind for good. Our slate was completely clean and clear of any cobwebs in the mind.

I have God's support and cooperation. I have a special niche for God in my heart. The scars of life's ups and downs were getting healed slowly. Life's new and fresh thinking will herald a new beginning, illuminating our lives with new light. The enlightened life's sun has risen in our heart, kindling our conscience with new energy.

When you lose your wealth you lose a lot; when you lose your best friend, you lose a lot more; however, when you lose courage, you lose your life. We need to change our thinking according to the changed situation.

We reached Dehradun Airport trying to sort out my tangled thoughts on the way. We were safe today, basking in the warmth of our family. Our first halt was Delhi as Nathudada (grandfather - nana) was waiting for us. His eyes welled up when he wrapped me in his arms. It was a momentous moment. I had the taste of coffee at the airport after a long time.

Bini and Nikhil Jijaji flew to Mumbai. Unfortunately, as their plane's tire got punctured, it got delayed. PG Uncle took a late flight to Mumbai.

When we were together in the troubled times, we had exchanged our cell phone numbers. The moment I charged my phone, I received a call from Dayanand. They had reached Haridwar after trudging through difficult terrain without food and water 24 hours. In spite of Jawans' help, their experience was quite horrifying. He fell sick and had to wait in Haridwar for treatment. Wasn't it a miracle? We were not having much trouble in the Dham as we were fortunate to breathe the air caressed by Shivji. However, the moment we reached the plains, we were down with health problems because of the pollution and the so called Kalyug '*air*'. The experience was horrifying in spite of the help from the brave hearts.

We reached Ahmedabad by evening where Ba, Bapuji, Kamleshbhai, all masis and mamis were waiting with bated breath. We got our blood and body checked by Dr. Kamleshbhai. I had my Khichadi and felt satiated and satisfied. I slept like a child.

The Happy End - Home

JUNE 25, 2013 DAY 21

Our flight to Mumbai was scheduled for the evening. After resting the whole day, by 6 in the evening we left for the airport. We were busy meeting relatives in Ahmedabad the whole day. We reached Mumbai, my hometown, by 8 pm. Shilpaben welcomed and greeted us with tears of joy at the airport. As we entered, all the members of our society were waiting to welcome us. Bharti burst firecrackers and welcomed us with a shower of flowers. We hugged each other tightly and cried. I felt very happy coming back home. They performed aarti and welcomed us home. Najuk bhabhi had decorated the passage with rose petals and diyas. We felt blessed to meet every one at home. It was like a Diwali celebration.

Our 15 days travel turned into 21 days of travails during which we went through the grind of sun and shade. We underwent hardships; on occasions, short of courage. Many people were responsible for our safe return. Our well-wishers' prayers were answered without their knowledge. Many relatives made vows for our safe return. Friends extended their help and advice. I thank all those who prayed for us and helped us come out unscathed.

AFTERMATH

After coming from Kedarnath many aspects of our life became clearer, imparting strength to understand, grasp, fathom and appreciate life. We are just puppets in the overall scheme of God. There is a personal touch even in the machinations of God which some are incapable of realising. Many understand the meaning of His touch and make their life worthwhile. Others are wasting their life by rowing the boat which is moored to the bank.

We can understand two things from the incident. We can prove it scientifically and religiously.

According to the scientists, due to the torrential rains on 16th June 2013, Saraswati River and Dudhganga Talav were overflowing resulting in increased flow in the canals. This caused comprehensive churning of the mud, sludge and slime on the river banks. This in turned cause it to sweep dirt and dregs, refuse and rubble, stones and pebbles along with it. Furthermore, the 7 ft ice formed on the mountains since many years started cracking and breaking into stones due to heavy rains. They started hurtling down through the Chorabati Talav, making their way to Kedarnath village and inundating it with mud and muck. The torrential rains which played havoc for seven days were unprecedented. The deluge was ghastly and horrific, something the villagers had never experienced before. It played havoc in Gaurikund, Rambada and many villages in Uttarakhand.

We were witness to terrible natural phenomenon for the first time. It was a classic example of Man facing Nature's fury due to his unbridled fiddling with ecological balance.

I could understand then, how nature donned a different look when it was disturbed by manmade forces. Human beings have destroyed all natural things for their personal gains. Roads constructed in haphazard style, new resorts and hotels built on fragile river banks and more than 70 hydroelectric projects in the watersheds of the state led to a "disaster waiting to happen". The tunnels built and blasts undertaken for the 70 hydroelectric projects contributed to the ecological imbalance in the state, with flows of river water restricted and the streamside development activity contributing to a higher number of landslides and more flooding.

We came to know later that the heavy rains resulted in large flash floods and massive landslides. Entire villages and settlements such as Gaurikund and the market town of Rambada, a transition point to Kedarnath, had been obliterated, while the market town of Sonprayag suffered heavy damage and loss of lives. Pilgrimage centres in the region, including Gangotri, Yamnotri, Kedarnath and Badrinath, the hallowed Hindu Char Dhams, are visited by thousands of devotees, especially after the month of May onwards. Over 70,000 people were stuck in various regions because of damaged or blocked roads. People in other important locations like the Valley of Flowers, Roopkund and Hemkund were stranded for more than three days. NH58, an important artery connecting the region, was also washed away near Jyotirmath.

It can also be proved religiously.

After we came back, we came to know that Dhari Mataji's Temple was again shifted on the 15th night. On 16th; the situation became bad. Each time the temple was shifted, calamity occurred, but the connection cannot be proved scientifically. The principles of Vastu Shastra-Science of Architecture and Construction and Geology also prove the phenomenon.

Shankarji and Dhari Devi are situated in south-west (head) and north-east (legs) as the flow of all the energy is directed towards north-east. Astrologically the direction is called as Guru direction (Ishan Shiv).

Kedarnath Jyotirling and Kalimath are situated in the north, which is the sign of relation between husband-wife, Shivji and Shakti. Kedarnath presiding in north manages to keep Devi presiding in the South contented. South direction is Mangal direction, which signifies anger, excitement and wrath; war means Kalimata. The place changed and the direction changed, changing the arithmetic. Kedarnath continuously quietens Kalimata. As he was incapable of reigning in Kalimata, Devi got enraged, resulting calamity.

We are unable to co-relate the two incidents. However it offers the proof of God's existence. During our trials and tribulations, we were each time made to realise the presence of God, doubling my faith in Him. We experienced His divinity, His fury, His coolness, His grandeur, His love and He imparted the ability to understand and realise. I consider myself blessed. Calamity is not a game of chance; only your karma will soften the intensity and severity of the shocks felt during the calamity. God always shows two ways; the choice of way will decide your fate.

When the Pandavas started climbing the golden ladder to Heaven, they saw their past karmas streaming before their eyes, and thus realized how they had become guilty of killings the innocents. Only Dharmaraja Yudhistir could climb the golden ladder. For his only mistake (lying about the death of elephant Ashwathama to Dronacharya) he had to suffer the anguish and grief of witnessing the death of his family members when he turned back.

Regarding the holy place as tourist spot, people unwittingly become partners in crime, kicking their chance for acquiring the golden ladder in the process.

Maybe as per the Creator, we fell short of performing our karmas. We hope God will give the requisite understanding to do good karmas, thereby opening the doors of Heaven.

It is almost a year since we suffered. My daily routine has been re-established. Office, movies, parties have restarted. There is a sense of satiation and equanimity behind each activity. The attitude towards competition, religion and donation has changed. Earlier we used to see the catastrophe as mere news item but now we feel one with the incident and so donate generously.

We can identify the hardships undergone by the sufferers. We become ever ready to help for a good cause. It lifts our spirits if we can bring back their smiles and twinkle in their eyes. We start realising the politics around us is petty. The incident which makes you feel sad teaches you something.

Dayanand is a tour operator. He also resumed his business. He lost 20 of his group members. Their faces and the sense of helplessness will be permanently etched in his psyche. His attitude is more towards ensuring happy faces and committing good deeds rather than earning profit alone. Richa lost her Mamas' families; two mamis, their two sons and nani - there is no news of them. Daily routine has started. However she continues to remember their faces. There was no warning that good times would end thus. Bad times come after good times but we never imagined that they would be so saddening. However God always thinks the best for everyone and hopefully opens the doors of Heaven to them

Some have lost their wives while some their parents, which has messed up and disturbed their lives. Some teenaged sons in our neighbourhood have also lost their parents. Their lives have grounded to a halt. The innocent sons do not have the bank details of their deceased parents. Overnight everything got grounded. The ability to rise from the ashes by the young brigade is commendable. Their friends and relatives due to their good deeds helped them in the hour of need and took upon themselves the responsibility of educating them. We have to help the needy in their hour of grief.

If you do a good deed there are many who would brand your act as selfish but that should not deter you from opting the path of benevolence. Today's act of goodness may be forgotten tomorrow but your act of kindness is registered in the books of Indradev, transforming into help when you need the most in emergency. You should strive to add more credits than debits in your accounts book with God.

I have learnt the art of living from the above experience. If we do good deeds our tomorrow will be automatically better. Whatever you do in your life, do it with friendliness, selflessly and truthfully, thereby achieving unusual peace. Result will come to complete fruition at a faster pace.

Glossary

Gaurikund 1.5 km: Inscribed on the milestone indicating the distance that it is 1.5 kilometre to Gaurikund. We chose the title of the book to indicate that we were so near yet too far from Gaurikund

Kedarnath: Kedarnath is a town located in the Indian state of Uttarakhand and has gained importance because of Kedarnath Temple in Rudraprayag district. The most remote of the four Char Dham sites, Kedarnath is located in the Himalayas, about 3,583 m (11,755 ft) above sea level near Chorabari Glacier, the head of river Mandakini, and is flanked by snow-capped peaks. The nearest road head is at Gaurikund, at a distance of 14 km.

Bholenathji: Bholenath (or Bolenath, Bhole Nath one of names of Hindu God Shiv.

Shivji: a Hindu deity, same as Shiv

Jawans: A junior soldier (especially an infantryman) this term usually covers all ranks below that of a Commissioned Officer in India.

Char Dham: (literally: 'the four abodes/seats') are the names of four pilgrimage sites in India that are widely revered by Hindus. It consists of Badrinath, Dwarka, Puri and Rameswaram. It is considered highly sacred by Hindus to visit Char Dham during one's lifetime. The Char Dham defined by Adi Sankaracharya consists of three Vaishnavite and one Shaivite pilgrimages.

The other pilgrimages sites in the Indian state of Uttarakhand viz. Yamunotri, Gangotri, Kedarnath, and Badrinath were known as Chhota (smaller) Char Dham to differentiate them from the bigger circuit of Char Dham sites, but after the mid-20th century, they have also been referred to as the Char Dham.

Kaliyug: Kali Yuga, in Sanskrit scriptures, is the "Age of Downfall", is the fourth stage of the world development that we are currently in.

Dekho: Watch, see Akshardham: A Hindu temple complex in Delhi, India. The complex displays millennia of traditional Hindu and Indian culture, spirituality, and architecture. The building was inspired and developed by Pramukh Swami Maharaj, the spiritual head of the Bochasanwasi Shri Akshar Purushottam Swaminarayan Sanstha (BSAPSS), whose 3,000 volunteers helped 7,000 artisans construct Akshardham.

Darshan: a Sanskrit term used for "visions of the divine" in Hinduism.

Devbhoomi: Uttarakhand was also the ancient Puranic term for the central stretch of the Indian Himalayas. Its peaks and valleys were well known in ancient times as the abode of gods and goddesses and source of the Ganges River. Today, it is often called "the Land of the Gods" (Dev Bhoomi) because of the presence of a multitude of Hindu pilgrimage spots. Uttarakhand is known as Dev Bhoomi from ancient times.

Yatra: In Hinduism and other Indian religions, generally means pilgrimage to holy places such as confluences of sacred rivers, places associated with Hindu epics such as the Mahabharata and Ramayana, and other sacred pilgrimage sites. Other meaning: 'journey', 'procession'

Barkot: It is located on the banks of the Yamuna river. Barkot is 126 km from the capital of Uttarakhand and 82 km from district headquarters Barkot on the way to Yamunotri and Gangotri Dham.

Yamnotri: is the source of the Yamuna River and the seat of the Goddess Yamuna in Hinduism. It is situated at an altitude of 3,293 metres (10,804 ft) in the Garhwal Himalayas and located approximately 30 kilometres (19 mi) North of Uttarkashi, the headquarters of the Uttarkashi district in the Garhwal Division of Uttarakhand,

Uttarkashi: meaning Kashi of the north, is a town in Uttarakhand, India. It is the district headquarters of Uttarkashi district. Uttarkashi is situated on the banks of river Bhagirathi at an altitude of 1352 m above sea level.

Gangotri: is a town in Uttarkashi district in the state of Uttarakhand, India. It is a Hindu pilgrim town on the banks of the river Bhagirathi and source of River Ganges. It is on the Greater Himalayan Range, at a height of 3,100m.

Guptakashi: is a fairly large town located at an elevation of 1,319 metres (4,327 ft) in the Kedar-khanda ('khanda' means "sector"), in Garhwal Himalayas of Rudraprayag district in Uttrakhand, India. It is famous for the ancient Vishwanath Temple - dedicated to god Shiva - similar to the one in Varanasi (Kashi). The name Guptakashi has legendary significance linked to the Pandavas, the heroes of the Hindu epic Mahabharata. Its religious importance is considered next to that of Varanasi, believed to be the most pious of all Hindu pilgrimage places.

Jungle Chatti: name of the area

Dehradun: is the capital city of the state of Uttarakhand in the northern part of India. Located in the Garhwal region, it is 236 km north of India's capital New Delhi. Dehradun is in the Doon Valley on the foothills of the Himalayas nestled between two of India's mightiest rivers — the Ganges on the east and the Yamuna on the west. The city is famous for its picturesque landscape and slightly milder climate and provides a gateway to the surrounding region. It is well connected and in proximity to popular Himalayan tourist destinations such as Missouri, Nainital and Auli and the Hindu holy cities of

Haridwar and Rishikesh along with the Himalayan pilgrimage circuit of Char Dham.

Ahmedabad

Bhagwan: God

Shankarji: same as Shiv

Dahi: Yogurt

Masi: Mother's sister

Jyotirlings: is a devotional object representing the god Shiva. Jyoti means 'radiance' and lingam the 'mark or sign' of Shiva, or a symbol of the pineal gland; Jyotir Lingam thus means the Radiant sign of The Almighty. There are twelve traditional Jyotirlinga shrines in India.

Nainital: is a popular hill station in Uttarakhand and headquarters of Nainital district in the Kumaon foothills of the outer Himalayas. Situated at an altitude of 2,084 metres (6,837 ft) above sea level.

Mahadevji: may refer to Shiva, a primary Hindu deity

Uttarakhand: is both the new and traditional name of the state that was formed from the hill districts of Uttar Pradesh, India. Literally North Country or Section in Sanskrit, the name of Uttarakhand finds mention in the early Hindu scriptures as the combined region of Kedarkhand and Manaskhand.

Haridwar: is an ancient city in Haridwar district of Uttarakhand, India. The River Ganges, after flowing for 253 kilometres (157 mi) from its source at Gaumukh at the edge of the Gangotri Glacier, enters the Indo-Gangetic Plains of North India for the first time at Haridwar, which gave the city its ancient name, Gangadwara.

Aarti: is a Hindu religious ritual of worship, a part of puja, in which light from wicks soaked in ghee (purified butter) or camphor is offered to one or more deities. Aartis also refer to the songs sung in praise of the deity, when lamps are being offered.

Har Ki Pedi: is a famous ghat on the banks of the Ganges in Haridwar. This revered place is the major landmark of the holy city of Haridwar. Literally, "Har" means "Lord Shiva" who is the god according to Shaivite Rishav school of Hindu theology, "Ki" means "of" and "Pedi" means "steps". Lord Shiva and Lord Vishnu are believed to have visited the Brahmakund in Har Ki Pedi in the Vedic times. There is a large footprint said to belong to Lord Vishnu on a stone wall.

Gangaji: is a trans-boundary river of Asia which flows through India and Bangladesh. The 2,525 km (1,569 mi) river rises in the western Himalayas in the Indian state of Uttarakhand, and flows south and east through the Gangetic Plain of North India into Bangladesh, where it empties into the Bay of Bengal. It is the third largest river by discharge.

The Ganges is the most sacred river to Hindus. It is also a lifeline to millions of Indians who live along its course and depend on it for their daily needs. It is worshipped as the goddess Ganga in Hinduism. Banaras, Allahabad, Kolkata etc are located on its banks.

Badrinath: is a holy town in Chamoli district in the state of Uttarakhand, India. It is the most important of the four sites in India's Char Dham pilgrimage and gets its name from the Holy temple of Badrinath.

Moksha: means emancipation, liberation or release. In the soteriological and eschatological sense, it connotes freedom from worldly woes, the cycle of death and rebirth. In the epistemological and psychological sense, moksha connotes freedom, self-realisation and self-knowledge

Shrinagar: Not to be confused with the summer capital of Jammu and Kashmir, Srinagar. Shrinagar is in Pauri Garhwal district in the Indian state of Uttarakhand.

Alaknanda: is a Himalayan river in the state of Uttarakhand, and one of the two head streams of the Ganges. In hydrology, the Alaknanda is considered to be the source stream of the Ganges on account of its greater length and discharge;[however, in Hindu mythology and culture, the other headstream, the Bhagirathi, is considered the source stream.

Sohanpapdi: is a popular Indian dessert. It is usually square in shape or served as flakes, and has a crisp and flaky texture. Its main ingredients are sugar, gram flour derived from chick peas, flour, ghee, milk and cardamom.

Ashiqi-2: Hindi movie

Kareena Kapoor: Hindi actress

Theplas: Theplas are an inherent part of Gujarati meals, and are used for regular meals, travelling and for picnics! Eaten with curds and chunda, theplas can be enjoyed hot or otherwise. Sometimes whole jeera or til can be added to enhance the flavour of theplas. You can even add other ingredients like methi and doodhi to this recipe, to add more variety to your menu.

Bhajiawala: The one who sells Bhajia. Also known as pakoras, made of potato or onions which are mixed in chickpea flour and fried. They are perfect snack for a cold, rainy day! Can be served with sweet-sour tamarind chutney.

DAY 2

Om Namah Shivay: is one of the most popular Hindu chants and the most important mantra in Shaivism. Its translation is "adoration (namas) to Shiva", preceded by the mystical syllable "Aum". Om Namah Shivaya mantra is sung by devotees in prayers and recited by yogis in meditation. It is associated with qualities of prayer, divine-love, grace, truth and blissfulness.

Sadan: House

Gulistan: garden

Swaminarayan Bhagwan: The Swaminarayan Sampraday is a Bhakti Sampraday founded by Bhagwan Swaminarayan on 31

December 1801 CE. It belongs to the Vaishnav tradition and represents the purest form of the Hindu religion. It focuses its faith on salvation through total devotion - bhakti - to the Supreme God developed through dharma, gyan and vairagya (righteousness, knowledge and detachment).

Ghanshyam Maharaj: another name of Swaminarayan Bhagwan

Krishna Leela and Raasleela: Raas dance is part of the traditional story of Krishna described in Hindu scriptures such as the Bhagwat Puran and literature such as the Gita Govinda, where he dances with Radha and her sakhis.

Gol-gappas or pani puri: is a popular street snack. It consists of a round, hollow puri, fried crisp and filled with a mixture of flavoured water ("pani"), tamarind chutney, chili, chaat masala, potato, onion and chickpeas. It is generally small enough to fit completely into one's mouth.

DAY 4

Hari's Dham: Shivji's place

Daal-bhaat: refers to a traditional meal which is popular in India. It consists of steamed rice and a cooked lentil soup called daal. It is our staple food.

Diyas: is an oil lamp, usually made from clay, with a cotton wick dipped in ghee or vegetable oils.

Sadhus: is an ascetic or holy person. Although the vast majority of sadhus are yogis, not all yogis are sadhus. The sadhu is solely dedicated to achieving moksha (liberation), the fourth and final ashram (stage of life), through meditation and contemplation of Brahman. Sadhus often wear saffron-coloured clothing, symbolising their sanyasa (renunciation).

Bhagwat: literally meaning Divine-Eternal Tales of The Supreme Lord, it is one of the maha (great) Puranic texts of Hinduism, with its focus on bhakti (religious devotion) to Supreme God Vishnu (Narayana), including the various avatars of Vishnu and primarily focusing on Krishna's life and pastimes of his complete incarnation.

Dharamsalas: is an Indian religious rest house. In Hindi, Dharma means religion, and shala means "sanctuary" hence dharamshala is a 'religious sanctuary' or rest-house for pilgrims.

DAY 5

Singdana: peanuts

Khakhra: Originating from the state of Gujarat, Khakhras are thin crackers made from mat bean, wheat flour and oil. It is served usually during breakfast. Khakhras are uniquely hand-made and roasted to provide a delicious, crunchy and healthy snack enjoyed with a selection of pickles and chutneys.

Chanas: is a legume. It is also known as gram or Bengal gram

Bisleri: branded mineral water

ParleG: branded glucose biscuits

Shastras: Scriptures

Krishnaji: A deity worshipped across many traditions of Hinduism in a variety of different perspectives. While many Vaishnava groups recognise him as an avatar of the god Vishnu; some traditions within Krishnaism consider Krishna to be Svayam Bhagavan, or the Supreme Being.

Mataji: also known as Mata Rani and Vaishnavi, is a manifestation of the Hindu Mother Goddess or Durga. The words "maa" and "mata" are commonly used in India for "mother", and thus are often used in connection with Vaishno Devi. Vaishno Devi Mandir is a Hindu temple dedicated to the Hindu Goddess, located at the Trikuta Mountains in Jammu and Kashmir.

Mussorie: a hill station

Makaai: roasted corn

Kachoris: is a spicy snack

DAY 6

Doli: palanquins

Doliwalas: Those who man the a doli

Horsewala: A person who manages horses.

Pittuwala: Porters (popularly called Pittus) for carrying luggage or for carrying young children who are afraid to or are too young to ride a horse, and light weighted old people.

Danda: a wooden stick used by the Indian police

Puja: A prayer ritual performed by Hindus to host, honour and worship one or more deities, or to spiritually celebrate an event. It also means reverence, honour, homage, adoration, and worship.

Bandhani: A type of tie-dye practiced mainly in the states of Rajasthan and Gujarat, a metre length of cloth can have thousands of tiny knots.

DAY 7

Gulab-jamuns: is a milk-solids based dessert, prepared by heating milk over a low flame for a long time until most of the water content has evaporated. These milk solids, known as khoya, are kneaded into a dough, sometimes with a pinch of flour, and then shaped into small balls and deep fried at a low temperature of about 148 °C. The balls are then soaked in a light sugar syrup flavoured with green cardamom and rosewater, kewra or saffron.

Bhabhi: brother's wife

Shrimad Bhagwat Gita: refer Bhagwat above

Rishi munis : In the Vedas the term Rishi denotes an inspired poet of Rigvedic hymns, who alone or with others invokes the deities with poetry. Post-Vedic tradition regards the Rishis as "sages" or saints.

DAY 8

Parshuramji: is the sixth avatar of Vishnu. He is son of Renuka and one of the saptarishis, Jamadagni. He lived during the end of Dvapara Yuga, and is one of the seven immortals or Chiranjivi, of Hinduism. He received parshu (axe) after undertaking intense penance to please Shiva, who in turn taught him the martial arts.

Bhagirath: was a great king who brought the River Ganges, personified as the river goddess Ganga, to Earth from the heavens.

Jata: matted hair (of Shankarji)

Gangadhar: Shankarji allowed the Gangaji through a strand of his matted hair. Gangaji then flowed humbly, gracefully and giving prosperity on her way to pataal. Thus the ancestors of Bhagirath were resurrected by the holy water of Gangaji. The posture holding the Gangaji in the matted hair is called Gangadhara Murthi.

Gaumukh: the terminus or snout of the Gangotri Glacier, from where Bhagirathi River originates, is one of the primary sources of the Ganges River. The place is situated at a height of 13,200 ft. It is one of the largest in the Himalayas with an estimated volume of over 27 cubic kilometres. It is a popular Hindu pilgrimage site, along with Gangotri, as well as trekking destination.

Gangajal: the holy water of Ganga is used in all religious ceremonies. If kept in the copper 'Kalash' in homes it gives holy vibrations and fights away evil and bad luck. It endows material prosperity and spiritual growth.

Abhisekh: Ceremonious holy bath of milk and water given to a deity. Anointing or consecrating.

Punditji: A learned man; a teacher; esp., a Brahmin well-versed in the Sanskrit language, and in the science, laws, and religion of the Hindus;

Chhole bature: is a combination of chole (spicy chick peas) and fried bread called bhatoora (made of maida flour)

Menka: In Hindu mythology, Menka is considered one of the most beautiful of the heavenly Apsaras. She was sent by Indra, the king of the Devas, to break the severe penance undertaken by Vishwamitra. Vishwamitra was one of the most respected and revered sages in ancient India.

Dhaba: is the name given to roadside restaurants. They are situated on highways and generally serve local cuisine, and also serve as truck stops.

DAY 10

Dhabawala: owner of Dhaba

Rotis: is flat bread, made from stoneground whole meal flour, traditionally known as atta flour.

Dhari Devi: is a temple on the banks of the Alaknanda River in the Garhwal Region of Uttarakhand. It houses the upper half of an idol of the goddess Dhari that, according to local lore, changes in appearance during the day from a girl, to a woman, and then to an old lady. The idol's lower half is located in Kalimath, where mata is prayed in Kali roop.

This shrine is one of the 108 Shakti sthals in India, as numbered by Shrimad Devi Bhagwat.

Ardhanareshwar: The other famous temple here is dedicated to Ardhanareshvara (a half man half woman form of Shiva and Parvati).

Kalimath: is a village which is regarded as a divine place and Shakti peeth. It lies at an altitude of around 6,000 feet (1,800 m) on the river Saraswati in the Himalayas. Kalimath is situated close to Ukhimath and Guptakashi. It is one of the "Siddha Peeths" of the region and is held in high religious esteem.

Rudra: is a Rigvedic deity, associated with wind or storm, and the hunt. The name has been translated as "the roarer" in the Rigveda. Rudra has been praised as the "mightiest of the mighty". The Shri Rudram hymn from the Yajurveda is dedicated to Rudra, and is important in the Saivism sect.

Swarup: Form taken by Shivji

Tandav: is a divine dance performed by the Hindu God Shiv.

DAY 11

Pandavas: In the Mahabharata, a Hindu epic text, they are the five acknowledged sons of Pandu, by his two wives Kunti and Madri. Their names are Yudhisthira, Bhima, Arjuna, Nakula and Sahadeva. All five brothers were married to the same woman, Draupadi. (Each brother also had multiple other wives.)

Dharmaraja: or Yudhisthira; eldest of Pandavas.

Pashupatinath: Nepal's most sacred Hindu shrine and one of the greatest Shiva sites, is located on the banks of the Bagmati River 5 kilometres north-east of Kathmandu Valley

Shivling: is a mountain at tapovan in the Gangotri Group of peaks in the western Garhwal Himalaya, near the snout of the Gangotri Glacier. It is 6 kilometres (4 mi) south of the Hindu holy site of Gaumukh (the source of the Bhagirathi River). Its name refers to its status as a sacred symbol of the God - Lord Shiva's Shiva Linga.

Chorabari Talav or Glacier: is a glacier in the Garhwal Himalaya region of the state of Uttarkhand in India. The glacier lies close to Kedarnath, an important destination for Hindu pilgrims. One of the glacier's two snouts is the source for the Mandakini River, a tributary of the Alaknanda river.

Swargarohini: is a mountain massif in the Bandarpunch Range of the Garhwal Himalaya. It consists of four separate peaks; Swargarohini is the main peak. Swargarohini derives its name from the legends associated with it: that its peak forms the path to heaven that was followed by Pandavas, Draupadi and their dog. According to legends it's believed that it is the only way one can go to heaven with the human body.

Vishnuji: is a popular Hindu deity, the Supreme God of Vaishnavism (one of the three principal denominations of Hinduism) and one of the three supreme deities (Trimurti) of Hinduism. He is also known as Narayana and Hari. As one of the five primary forms of God in the Smarta tradition, He is conceived as "the Preserver or the Protector" within the Trimurti, the Hindu Trinity of the divinity.

Kachha Road: semblance of road Adi Sankaracharya: One of the most revered Hindu philosophers and theologians from India from early 8th century, he consolidated the doctrine of Advaita Vedanta.

Shamiana: Shamiana is a popular Indian ceremonial tent shelter or awning, commonly used for outdoor parties, marriages, feasts etc. Its side walls are removable. The external fabric can be multi-coloured or can hold exquisite designs. The four corners are supported by wooden poles.

Shringar Darshan: The first hour darshan is called shringara. Shrinathji is dressed carefully from head to foot, and a garland of flowers is placed around his neck. A Mukhiya holds a mirror in front of him so that he can satisfy himself that he is well dressed. This is his play hour like that of any other child, and he is offered dry fruits and sweets representing food brought to him by his beloved gopis.

Draupadiji: wife of Pandavas

Puranas: Scriptures

Kailashnathji: Shankarji

Garhwal: Garhwal Kingdom consisted of the present day Tehri Garhwal district and most of the Uttarkashi district. Garhwal Kingdom acceded to the Union of India in August 1949.

Mandakini River: is a tributary of the Alaknanda River. Mandakini originates from the Chorabari Glacier near Kedarnath. Mandakini is fed by Vasukiganga River at

Sonprayag. Mandakini joins Alaknanda at Rudraprayag. Alaknanda then proceeds towards Devaprayag where it joins with Bhagirathi River to form the Ganges River. Mandakini river flows along NH-107 in Rudraprayag district and turns violent during monsoon, often destroying parts of highway and adjoining villages.

Bhairav Roop Darshan

Tandav Nrutya is a divine dance performed by the Hindu god Shiva. Shiva's Tandava is described as a vigorous dance that is the source of the cycle of creation, preservation and dissolution.

Bhutafala

Natraja Darshan: Lord Nataraja performs cosmic dance

DAY 12

Hei Maheshwar.

Hei Ashutosh: instant gratification provider

Hei Anantdrushtiwala: perennial visionary

Dhyandeep: Icon of Meditation and Concentration

Rambada: a place between Kedarnath and Gaurikund.

Trilokpati: Lord of the three worlds

Kalima

Palanhar: The one who protects us

Divya Drishti Shivji: Divine Visionary

Krishna- Arjun

Jhuggies: huts

Shantywala: Owner of shanty

Hotelwala: Owner of hotel

Anant Drishti: Perennial Visionary

Trilok: three worlds

Digambar: the whole world is his costume

Dohas: is a form of self-contained rhyming couplet in poetry. This genre of poetry first became common in Apabhraṃśa and was commonly used in Hindi and Urdu poetry. Among the most famous dohas are those of Sarahpa, Kabir, Rahim, Tulsidas, Jamiluddin Aali, and Surdas.

DAY-13

Avyayprabhu and Avanashi: Imperishable, Indestructible.
Bhudev: God of Nature
Khichadi: is an Indian preparation made from rice and lentils (dal). Khichri is commonly considered to be a comfort food.

DAY 14

Kapalin
Vinashak: the destroyer
Bhairav avatar or Bhairavnath, sometimes known as Kala Bhairava, is a Hindu deity, a fierce manifestation of Shiva associated with annihilation. The origin of Bhairava can be traced to the conversation between Brahma and Vishnu recounted in the Shiv Mahapuran where Vishnu asked Brahma who is the supreme creator of the Universe. Arrogantly, Brahma told Vishnu to worship him, he being the supreme creator.
Bhairav Chatti :
Jiju/Jijaji: Sister's husband :
Gayatri Mantra: is a highly revered mantra of the Vedic tradition. Just like all the Vedic Mantras, the Gayatri Mantra is considered not to have an author and like all other mantras is believed to have been revealed to a Brahmarshi, in this case Brahmarshi Vishvamitra. This is a Vedic Sanskrit verse from a hymn of the Rigveda (3.62.10). Gayatri is the name of the meter in which the verse is composed.
Mrityunjay mantras or Triambakji Path: "Great Death-conquering Mantra", also called the Triambakam Mantra, is a verse of the Rigveda (RV 7.59.12). It is addressed to

Triambaka, "the three-eyed one", an epithet of Rudra, later identified with Shiva. The verse also recurs in the Yajurveda (TS 1.8.6.i; VS 3.60)

Shlokas : shloka is a couplet. Each hemistich (half-verse) of 16 syllables, composed of two Padas of eight syllables, can take either a pathyā ("normal") form or one of several vipulā ("extended") forms.

DAY 15

Nepalis: inhabitants of Nepal

Darbar: Court

Pawan Hans: Airlines which operates helicopter services.

Daane daane pe likkha hain khaanewale ka naam: Every grain is assigned to the person who eats it.

Maharajshri: Pundit or Brahman who performs pujas

Raam bolo bhai raam: words chanted while taking the dead body for cremation

Swaroop: Form

DAY 16

Triveni Sangam: the "confluence" of three rivers. Sangama is the Sanskrit word for confluence. The point of confluence is a sacred place for Hindus. A bath here is said to flush away all of one's sins and free one from the cycle of rebirth.

Puris: Puris are perhaps one of the most well-known and versatile of Indian foods made from wheat flour and deep fried. It can be served as a snack or a meal depending on the accompanying items. However, it is important to know the right way of making puris, so that they come out nice and fluffy and without too much oil.

Boondi: is a Rajasthani snack food made from sweetened, fried chickpea flour. Being very sweet, it can be stored for a week or so. Due to the need for preserving food in arid regions of Rajasthan, boondi laddu is preferred. There is also a savoury version, called Khara or Tikha.

Frooti: Indian candied fruit drink

Biharis: inhabitants of Bihar

Chaat: is a term describing savoury snacks, typically served at road-side tracks from stalls or food-carts. With its origins in Uttar Pradesh chaat has become immensely popular

Master of Ghost: another name of Shivji

The Protector of Ghost: another name of Shivji

The Moon Carrier: another name of Shivji

DAY 17

Bhuteshwar: Protector of Ghost

Gitaji: literally meaning The Song of the Bhagwan, often referred to as simply the Gita, is a 700-verse Hindu scripture that is part of the Hindu epic Mahabharata.

DAY 18

Lungi: also known as a sarong, is a traditional garment worn around the waist

Aghoribaba

DAY 19

Idli

AFTERMATH

Saraswati River

Dudhganga Talav

Vastu Shastra

Nani: maternal grandmother

Masi: Mother's sister

Mami: wife of maternal uncle

Indradev

Roopkund

Hemkund

Jyotirmath